THE FOES OF

GOD

By

L.A. Kendrick

PAPERBACK ISBN: 978-969-2792-07-3

EBOOK ISBN: 978-969-2592-08-0

Table Of Contents

Intro

H ELL, most of you think of it as a place of fantasy, smoke, and mirrors, a metaphor meant to put fear into us in order for an oppressive form of control to rule. A control that is clearly out dated in the minds of many, and serves no purpose in today's society. In today's society up until a few months ago, a vast majority said that GOD was dead. All that has changed, for what has been unleashed on Earth due to the Insurrections against GOD clearly has been wiped from the minds of all on the planet. Doing what we want, without thought or regard for not man's law but nature's natural order has brought us to what will be the eradication of all that is known or ever will be. Just a little patience, a small degree of understanding, that some lines should never be crossed, could have prevented all of this. I was brought up to respect all things natural, and question or stay away from things that were to the contrary. In order to achieve a higher spirituality, one must apply discipline to his life, as no one is perfect it is the job of the man to always challenge the mind, the body, as well as the spirit. We have to descend into the nightmare of modern man as well as any civilization that existed before us. This place is more terrifying than any could ever imagine, here there are no second chances, no I'm sorry, and no I am ready to believe now. For here in this place, physical life is a past condition that should have been handled in life when the opportunity was readily available. Every fabric, every atom has a horrible life of torture and torment of its own. I would say unto anyone that is weak of spirit, or squeamish not follow us into this journey because this place is full of dread. Hope has never known this place, we bring the hope with us, but make no mistake this is a place where GOD had cast out his most beloved generals of heaven. For their disobedience, this is their eternal domain; his law does not change man does. If we go back on what he decrees as wrong, never coming to the mind that repentance is then necessary once a wrong within us is identified, then this is our final place. Each person will face their own personal HELL, for eternity each second experiencing unimaginable pain, and torment. This is not group therapy; there is a 50/50 chance that GOD is real and a 50/50 chance he is not. We are currently in Hell, which means that you can't have one without the other. Plus there is one truth; we all have to die and that is not the time to believe in Allah, GOD, or The Great Spirit. We have lost many on this journey into a place that all religious groups have spoken about in detail. A place that is beyond a moral compass; I will never question the power of truth again. I will continue to redeem and repent for my soul, so if you have any wrongs that you need to right, now is the time. Sin is sin, we all need to recognize them, but I fear that it is too late. Hell has spilled over into our world; it is the Rapture as the Great Spirit foretold. I will do my part to show that there is some good left within the human spirit. Who am I? Cinder Hawk, soul tracker of the once mighty Apache nation. I am sorry to say with all things current, we have officially in our willful ignorance become "THE FOES OF GOD!"

Chapter 1

"ROT"

A.k.a *Death*

1 3 degrees 36'N, 40 degrees 40'E, 1300 hours Zulu time Erta Ale volcano, Ethiopia. 13 days ago we came seeking entrance, here at the southernmost pit. Earth's first and oldest gateway to Hell, when we arrived we had no bloody idea of the hideous boogers that were scurrying out from the rim of the volcano's entrance. We wiped them all out but more horrors await us. By all accounts, the seals have all been broken thanks to Osiris, and the Gem of Chaos, the demons of Hell are no longer bound. We have come to find a way to lessen the power of the new horsemen of the apocalypse. They have presented themselves with new more modern names, but nonetheless are equally as powerful. They are Rot, Aka Death; Pathogen, Aka Pestilence; Combaticus, Aka War; and Atrophy, Aka Famine. If we can retrieve what we need here it just might bloody well give us a chance, the only chance we could have. We started with 12; our Afar local guides have been killed they were followers of the mighty spirit of OGUN. We asked for a few warriors as their tribe is tasked with guarding the hidden treasures of King Mansa Musa the

1st of the Malian Empire of West Africa, born in the time period somewhere in the 1280's he is considered the richest man in recorded history, once they understood the gravity of the situation they came without hesitation. Only four of us remain after one perilous pitfall after another those poor blokes were valiant to the end. Cinder Hawk, who is somewhat of a Native American mystic warrior, Bish bah, a Soul Sprite that tracks and locates lost souls, Outrage, and I Warcast. I knew to allow only those who had a firm grasp on the true concept of good and evil to accompany us. The strangest thing that has me completely vexed, some of our mates had seemingly vanished without any fighting. One moment they would be standing getting their bearings the next, poof gone in a whisk! We must continue on perils await.

"Never did I imagine this to be so sullen a place, the deeper we travel the more I'm glad that my training was so intense. My tribal Shaman prepared me well" Cinder Hawk says.

"I agree even with the many runes, marks of protection, and holy relics. This place is abhorrent to say nothing of the sort" Warcast replies with a British accent.

"We must not stop our quest will surely bring us a victory!" Outrage says.

"What makes your big blue butt so sure, this is hell the end of the universe, all dimensions, the place where all the bad unrepented sentient life goes. We got you big dumb humans to blame for all of this mess, well maybe not you weirdo" Bish bah says.

"I've done much research on magical creatures of your planet but never had I come across a sprite with an Afro" Outrage replies as he tries to lighten the mood.

"Well that's funny coming from a big blue, double pony-tailed Genie-looking thing, what exactly are you?" Bish bah says as he darts back and forth in front of the face of Outrage looking to figure him out. He flies without wings, he is a being of pure good and magic, but you wouldn't be able to tell that by his sharp tongue. He is given flight by a burning light blue flame that engulfs him.

They all laugh at the comment made by Bish bah, who lands on Cinder Hawk's shoulder as they descend to one of the final levels of Hell the two have been a team for most of Cinder Hawk's life. Warcast looks at the map given to him by the recently killed guide. They must travel through the "Corridor of Corinthians", and make their way to "The forest of the unforgiven". There at the end of the forest before the final "Lair of Lucifer," will they finally be done with the journey. But they suddenly notice blue glowing footprints leading to "The Corridor of Corinthians" Bish bah knows exactly who they belonged to!

"Bless my soul do you bums know who made these footprints?" Bish bah asks. They all look puzzled without an answer for they are unsure, who could traverse Hell and leave such a beacon of light and hope in such a dark dreary place.

"Please, by all means, Bish bah enlighten us mate!" Warcast replies.

"Well, my good fellows you all are witnessing the legendary footprints of the Archangel that patrols this particular level of Hell. I thought that it was just a myth even among my people, none have seen what you are seeing". Bish bah says with renewed focus.

"Are you sure?" Warcast asks as the sight of true power and glory overwhelms him, and also shows him that he has much to learn from the Light Lords.

"Of course, I'm sure this is the most powerful energy ever this is the path of the Archangel that guards this level of Hell. He was assigned this post to prevent the demons here, well that was here in check. I'm a being of pure good and light I'm made of the stuff, I may joke a bit but this energy is where all good and pure beings throughout the cosmos are born. Just in smaller doses, my friends are the only living beings to ever see this spectacle. Behold my friends, these are the footprints of the Archangel Zabaniyah!" Bish bah replies and all present take a knee and pay respect before the lit path of Zabaniyah, and at that moment they realize that Bish bah speaks the truth.

They come to their feet and check their gear, as they look toward the path that must be taken. It is like nothing the living has ever seen before danger lurks in every corner. It is the stuff of nightmares, these four have unyielding faith and they will need it to continue. As they move to the "Corridor of Corinthians", the ground seems to become flesh and alive. Low growls and moans fill the air, Warcast takes a deep breath as he motions the rest to move forward.

"If we move in quietly, I believe that we stand a better chance of not attracting attention. We should proceed slowly, and with stealth, I fear we shall only progress into more difficulty as we travel to "The lair of Lucifer!" Warcast says as he looks on.

"I don't believe that he is here, no Archangels are here either. Whatever that thing is that accompanied the four horsemen, has cleaned house and he has got to be pretty powerful to wipe out Lucifer. There is no trace of his evil energy and most of the demons have been killed look at them scattered all over this place!" Bish bah replies flying back and forth surveying the area.

"So this will be easier than it would appear?" Outrage adds while gripping his golden hammer.

"No, do not be fooled there is someone or something left here trying to lay a claim as the next king of hell. I can sense the evil, and also something that is neither good nor evil". Cinder Hawk says.

The faithful four continue towards the opening, the sky is an eternal black and red flame-filled tapestry. While souls of the dammed float across and cover the horrid sky canvas. They shriek in agony as they are tormented for sins long ago and continue in an unending nightmarish buffet of delight for the demon wardens of hell. The mortals begin to feel weak but Bish bah and Warcast seem to be unaffected because of the divine nature that is their bloodline.

Cinder Hawk begins a chant that would strengthen the spiritual resolve of he and Outrage. They press into the Corridor of Corinthians they are but a few feet in then the walls and the very ground begin to come to life and assault them. Faces and hands of the dammed begin to speak in agony, covered in bile and blood begging for salvation griping for the righteous light they once had in life. Attempting to siphon off the life forces that accompany our travelers.

Some faces are slime-covered, some burned, others are decayed, while most are scarred or deformed beyond belief. They all seek a way to escape by any means possible, and as they start to tear themselves from the walls; they block the passage in an attempt to usurp our warriors' life force. Giving a new meaning to the term misery loves company, they intend on making our heroes stay in eternal torment with them. But our heroes must reach the end of this narrow passage if they have any hope of a possible solution.

"These people had no honor nor respect in life, so they surely do not have any in death. Why do they not just accept their fate, they chose not to believe in a higher power, when they had life. Now they scream and beg for a second chance in death!" Cinder Hawk says, as his brow becomes wrinkled with disappointment at the sight of it all.

"I have had several conversations, with young blocks about why would GOD punish me for loving who I chose to love or how I live my life. I would say quite often, he gives you free will to do, as you will. That does not mean that there are no consequences to our actions, so you make these at your own risk. I wish they could now see, what we see, this place is beyond the darkest imagination. This is what awaits all who want to do, what one wants without, the thought of spiritual limitation and no fear of divine retaliation." Warcast responds.

"Yeah you humans are dumb, you think you are the center of the universe. As if you created GOD, even you, you big blue whatever you are. Your people are guilty also of trying to become gods, don't stand there silent and act like you don't know what I'm talking about!" Bish bah says as Warcast looks at Outrage with an eyebrow raised, wondering what Bish bah is speaking of.

But this is truly a conversation for another time because the lost souls are trying to hold them all in place. For they are now all minions of Hell, forced to do, as the place requires them. In order to collect more souls, Hell has many tricks. This place knows that its final hour is at hand, and intends to take as many souls with it as possible. The arms and hands of the unholy reach out grabbing and clawing at the group as they try to press forward!

"Their wailing is so intense, they are truly tortured in this place. Now they reach and grab gnashing at us. I cannot seem to break free; they hold us with sheer desperation!" Cinder Hawk says as they are being pulled into the walls to join the damned. For once you are pulled into these walls, you will be forever joined with the eternal damned.

"Solenco, Faha doom, Rah ha, by the Light Lords you will release us and remain silent. You have by all accounts chosen your paths for this after life we shall not be made victims of your foul deeds!" Warcast responds as he chants an ancient spell taught by one of his many mentors "The Light Walkers."

The foul souls of long ago recoil back into the sides of the corridor. They become frozen once again back into place, only slow drips of ectoplasmic mucous drips from the hands, and faces that still protrude out cemented outward. The agony of their condition is etched permanently on their faces due to the powerful spell Warcast has provided. They continue on.

"Well, that was a bit of fun, hey mates?" Warcast says while the rest look around amazed at the paralyzed evil that had just moments ago tried to take them.

"Not bad for a human elf hybrid, so it's true you trained with the divine ones. Only they know those kinds of powerful spells to battle the dark lighters. Consider yourself fortunate, my friends we have a powerful force of good with us, not as good as me of course but not bad!" Bish bah brags.

They leave the passage and can see the entrance to "The Forest of the fallen flesh". There all of the most despicable crimes against GOD and man are tormented. Next to the level of Lucifer, there is no more abominable place in existence. If you are here, then you are beyond reprieve. The quartet ventures in further, as an eerie thick fog begins to cover the ground. Just as it does, they notice that the ground has taken on a peculiar texture. It is flesh; hell has woven a tapestry, and the skin of countless fallen souls make up this vast grotesque road leading into "The Forrest of the fallen flesh."

They can see that part of where they need to go has a bizarre fire burning eternal on some of the trees. Just then the ground is completely covered by the menacing thick fog. The fog smells of Sulfur, and Brimstone, making the air thick and hard to breathe but still they press on. The stench is almost overwhelming as it also momentarily burns their eyes. Ever vigilant, these brave souls trek further as the fog seems to stick to all but Bish bah, and Warcast is walking on the top of the fog to the shock of the others.

"Just there over that small Fischer, the one that is spewing what appears to be blood. Take care not to let it get on your person!" Warcast says as he times the sequential spurts of the liquid as he crosses over the crack in the surface.

"What have we done, we have condemned this planet and all other things in the heavens to this fate?" Cinder Hawk responds as he takes in the surroundings that no living thing has ever seen before.

"I would have to agree, some of what I see looks nothing like what you see!" Outrage adds, he then looks around trying to make sense of what the others are seeing versus what he is seeing.

"By that statement what do you mean?" Warcast asks.

"What he means is that everyone's perception of Hell is theirs alone, he is seeing Hell in whatever planet that he is from. All the stories, his culture's beliefs, he is looking at it from the horrors that his people see it. I gotta ask though since you show no emotion, what's it like? You seem to be elevated in anxiety, is this some kind of weird alien fear?" Bish bah questions.

"You could say that this is a realm that my people and all in the universe fear, even as well they should. I believe that I may have earned a spot here in this place," Outrage says looking downward remembering what he did in his home world.

"Nah if that were the case you would have been gobbled up. This place doesn't have favorites, you big blue whatever you are" Bish bah warns as they move ever closer.

The ground has become bumpy and sticky as if they are walking through rocks and duct tape. Unfortunately, they cannot see the ground, but Warcast is about to reveal a shocking fact. Something has the feet of Outrage, and Cinder Hawk so tight that not even Outrage can pull his foot free.

"I cannot move, the poisonous fog is so thick that I do not know what has such a firm grasp on me." Outrage says as he begins to stomp the ground with his remaining free foot, trying desperately to free himself.

"We need to free them fast, nothing here stationary lasts long!" Bish bah yells as he tries to pull Cinder Hawk up by the arm.

Warcast then focuses and casts a spell causing the wind to clear the area's ground. As the ground is cleared, the terrible revelation is revealed as to what is holding them. The ground is covered by thousands of eyes, big, and small of all colors. Two have closed around the feet of Cinder, and Outrage the eyes begin to blink with flashing ominous black lights. The flashing is like millions of camera shutters, and it causes all present to go blind, divine and mortal alike.

"I CAN'T SEE THESE LIGHTS HAVE ROBBED ME OF MY SIGHT!" Cinder Hawk yells he begins to reach out as if trying to find his way.

"One of you bums had better do something because what's coming next could punish us all!" Bish bah says.

The flashing black light makes them all see sins of their pasts, horrifically magnify exponentially. It will slowly make them break down, with grief and agony. For Bish bah, however, being a force of good has no such vices, but he is still robbed of his sight. They must be made to see that this is an illusion or all will be trapped here. Seeing hell firsthand is only making the struggle to let go of past sins impossible. For this is the place where one goes when sins have not been absolved. Outrage falls to one knee, while Warcast grabs his head screaming, I have failed Cinder Hawk says as he grabs his chest as if he has lost something dear and close to his heart.

"Hey you bums need to snap out of it, I can't see but I can tell you that what you see is not real. Somebody had better act really fast before they come!" Bish bah yells.

Cinder Hawk stumbles to stand, with his foot still caught in the slimy closed eye. He begins to chant he is an ordained priest within his tribe; the mental burdens of the black light that has plagued his teammates begin to lose their potency. Warcast shakes off the effect and begins to call on the light from all that is pure and divine. All the eyes on the ground that they walk upon, begin to close the holy chants that are causing them much pain. Cinder Hawk has gained momentum; his chants are renewing all of the heroes present with renewed vitality.

"Outrage, does your hammer cancel supernatural energies as well as regular magic?" Cinder Hawk asks.

"Indeed it does!" Outrage replies eagerly to regain his sight.

"When I stop chanting strike the ground, Warcast then you release the purity light. It will free us from this stretch of hell!" Cinder Hawk says.

"You shall have it let us end these bogeys that wish to rob us of our souls!" Warcast yells, and at that moment Cinder Hawks chanting stops!

"NOW, OUTRAGE STRIKE THE GROUND FORCE THE EYES OPEN!" Cinder Hawk shouts.

The mighty Outrage strikes the ground with such impact that a shock wave ripples through the flesh-covered ground of hell. Every eye on the hell-filled ground is forced open. Freeing Cinder Hawk and Outrages feet from their immobilization. Warcast is primed to make his move.

"WARCAST NOW, WE ARE RELEASED BRING THE LIGHT!" Cinder Hawk yells.

"BY THE DIVINE LIGHT INCARNATE, ILLUMINUS, PORTA, DECRECENDO!" Warcast shouts as he stomps the surface on which they stand. Light explodes from his body, blinding the horrid eyes that wish to rob them of life. So brilliant is the flash that every eye on the hellish surface is dried up and reduced to dust or encased in stone. Some of the eyeballs explode with sulfur-smelling fluid released onto the surface. Vision is restored to the warriors, and they know that what was to follow was a fate worse than death. They have prevailed for now.

"Great job you blue-tinted whatever you are, guess you are useful who knew?" Bish bah taunts Outrage.

"The bothersome thing is that by no means does this get any easier, over that small hill is our last endeavor. Let us tally on, and end this nightmare quickly!" Warcast says.

The group moves over the hill, trying not to notice the sinister ghostlike, phantoms that float around them. Seemingly they fill the area and are more active now since they are the only living things in the realm. They want to feed off the life force energy that our boys are giving off.

"They really seem to want us bad, but cannot for we are protected by the Great Spirit!" Cinder Heart says trying to reassure himself.

"All here are but tortured souls, former shells of what they were, as humans." Outrage adds as he seems to have pity, but Bish bah however has no such sympathy.

"They had their chances in life they choose this path, now they know that hell is real. Too bad they can't let their loved ones or the living know without dragging them here too. That's what they'd do misery loves company, I don't feel that bad for em. Free will and all it's a gift!" Bish bah explains zipping back and forth through the air.

He then reveals to the crew their final destination, and as they come to the top of the hill and descend to the bottom. They see sights that totally stop them in their tracks, because now what was written in Corinthians has just been made a shocking hard fact. Terror grips them all except Bish bah, he has no fear of being born into divinity, and this place holds no terror for him.

"This my friends and you big blue whatever you are is what awaits us, there is no mercy in that place. Behold, "The forest of the fallen flesh", one warning does not interfere in what ya gonna see in there. Those that are there have outright earned a spot on the starting lineup which is hell. Bish bah says as he leads them on.

Warcast can only muster two profound words.

"OH, DEAR!"

Chapter 2

"The forest of the fallen flesh"

Finally, the quartet has made it to the forest, the stench, and smell have made this a vision that none present will ever forget. Flesh rotting, the moaning of the damned and reprobate flow through the layout. Cries of help me, forgive me permeate around the lot. Requests that when their souls were occupied able bodies were not made. Only through pain and suffering in today's time, does man call on the creator, only then is he willing to believe! But that is an argument reserved for another day. The entrance is filled with creatures unseen before; the trees seem to be alive with unholy evil. Each branch has demonic birds, with wings that look as if they were made of spandex. Each monstrous beak displays an unnerving grin with torn bits of flesh as they probe each member. Trees ancient and despicable burn with hellfire. Further down range, they can see the infamous river bile as specters float over the repulsive river as if looking for an escape route. Soon they come upon the sins of man, and the torturing of the flesh and lost souls by demons. Let the edification begin.

"Whatever you see here, I warn you do not interfere. This place is for their wrongs this is their hell, no heroic crap because you like many others that walked in your shoes tried to help them in life. This is what they wanted." Bish bah says.

The moans of agony become louder as they penetrate the sulfuric fog, but this time is different. Agony moans are accompanied by crackling, bone-chilling laughing, now they can see where it is all coming from. Demons, more specifically torture demons, and they are taking pleasure in what they are doing, with great pleasure. The crew is witness to cruelty beyond, what any living mortal can conceive. The demons look at them, but only for a moment then it's back to business.

First, on the list of the damned, they have a huge rotisserie style spic over a crack in the surface that has hellfire bellowing up to serve as a heat source to burn eternal the souls they have. Each section of the wooden spindle of death has a body impaled on it. The gigantic stick has penetrated the lost souls, through the rectum and mouth. Each of the damned on the stick has their hands and feet tied and bound unable to move no matter how hard they struggle to free themselves. As they wait in line for their turn, several scream so loud that it sends proverbial ice through the veins of the onlookers. The demons dance around the fallen as the fire burns their souls, they howl in pleasure. One demon turns the handle rotating the damned over the open flame, while another takes a huge ladle from a cauldron and bastes the burning body with a disgusting white fluid.

So foul is the smell that, the mortals become dizzy and disoriented. Outrage vomits as he falls down on all fours; the amount of spew is enormous. It catches the attention of one of the demons; it quickly scurries over to collect the discharge of blue bodily fluids. The demon does not miss a drop; with lightning speed, it gathers the spit strings that hang from the staggered Outrage's mouth. It adds all that it has gained to the cauldron from which it covers the soul with the surrounding demonic dirt, skin, and all.

"Now that is just nasty, you big blue whatever you are. I'm gonna start calling you Bobby Hurley! Even your insides are blue it seems." Bish bah taunts.

"What is that Bish bah, what is that vile fluid it even adds more filth to that container?" Cinder Hawk asks.

"It's bile, from the River Bile over there, it's used to further defile and mark those that are unrepented. It's written in 1 Corinthians.6, Leviticus 18:22, 20:13, Romans Chapter-1 didn't anybody pay attention in bible school. All here, Murders, Rapist, Alcoholics, Drug users, Adulters, Fornicators, Hate Mongers, and oh yes even Homosexuals that you see tied to that contraption. No matter what you people say or think, it too is a sin still, what don't look at me I didn't write the book or make the laws?" Bish bah says as they all look at him Outrage begins to stand.

Strange as it sounds all the demons at the hellfire burning, stop and listen to his sermon, and they giggle in delight.

"So the Dark Duke really did his job on humanity, truly his greatest trick is making mankind believe that he doesn't exist. And you bums all fell for it, as you can see HELL DOES EXIST"? Bish bah explains.

"He never had me fooled, for all my life I have tried to make a difference willing to make the ultimate sacrifice. In my tribe he was often spoken of, as was the Great Spirit" Cinder Hawk replies.

"Nor had he I, I have seen countless hells throughout my time. I have dedicated my life to righteous things. I have made mistakes and prayed for forgiveness, but if humanity could see this then rest assured they would think twice about all actions!" Warcast says.

The demons continue to laugh and turn to administer more punishment, and the horror show takes off once again. Humans run down the past while demons have what appear to be water hoes that shoot out hellfire. Burning them, knocking them to the ground as they writhe in pain trying to put themselves out. Obviously, that's not going to happen because this is eternal payment for past indiscretions. Saturated by the hellfire, the souls are burned to smoldering ash.

Others are being chased by demons, but not just a normal chase these demons have unleashed the dogs, not just any dog hellhounds to attack the damned. They run and then the demons simply point in the direction of the runners, and the huge monstrous beasts are off. Their demon masters release the hellfire chains that hold the hell-spawned beast at bay. Running down their prey, the attack is brutal as they rip into the seemingly still human flesh. They rip off arms, legs, heads, and some are swallowed whole, screams fill the dark hopeless area. After they have been captured killed, and eaten they are regurgitated through the mouth or released through the rectum as feces. Slowly they are reformed, back into their original forms, and the process is repeated over and over again for eternity or however long humanity has left. Others have smoldering brimstone, thorn-riddled snakes, and broken branches shoved into every sexual orifice. The soul-shattering screams continue as several are strapped down upon boulders, but they have what appears to be tubes forced down their throats, bile is poured and forced down their throats. The damned try to cough the putrid liquid out but to no avail. More of the damned are injected with needles of hellfire and vapor demons; they rip through the souls causing mass hallucinations and unbearable pain and suffering. Several hang on trees, by the arms, neck, and feet as demons with thorny whips of hellfire savagely beat them, while demons dance in circles mocking them. The screams echo from days of the old American past, as the sins of the fathers are carried on for generations. As creatures that resemble insects eat the flesh from the tortured, demonic red-eyed birds and bats of this realm eat the eyes, ears, and lips of the fallen captured dammed. The demons shout at them in an unspeakable language, cries of forgiveness are only amusing to the demons fueling their tortuous rampage. The beatings are savage and don't stop as unholy flesh is torn and ripped from the bodies of the fallen their blood-beaten body covers the surface. Groups of the fallen are forced to bend over rocks, while large goat-faced demons rape them relentlessly some are clawed and scratched as they are being raped. Some try to rise up from the demoralizing excruciating assault, but the demons only force their heads down violently against the boulders. Men in business suits, and law enforcement officials, alike are caught in a wind tunnel of sharp-edged money, screams of the vile try to cut deals even here in hell. The only cuts they receive are eyes first then across the body, cutting veins arteries, and bone, as they bleed out the process, begins again, mimicking the foul deeds they pushed in their mortal lives. The pain here is legendary as is written, the wounds heal and the process repeats over and over.

"I truly never wish to be on the side of this world, I have no words for the horror I feel!" Outrage says as he clutches his enchanted golden hammer.

"Well, they are here because they earned this, and don't say to me that I'm judging. Judging would be me saying the Whopper is better than the Big Mac, now that's judging. This place my friends was a promise for those who embraced the trickster the King of Hell!" Bish bah replies.

"I do believe with all that is taking place on the surface above us, humanity surely has a different perspective on the hereafter!" Warcast says.

"Well just hang loose, we are almost there, see that cross-section in the distance? That's our final point what you seek is just over there in the center, just keep moving and no matter what ya see DO NOT INTERFERE everything here is built on lies!" Bish bah responds.

More grotesque sounds surround them as if they were walking through a haunted house at an amusement park. The passing by of a trail with demons leading hordes of humans is a replay that when in life these individuals broke treaties and forced Native Americans to be relocated. Here in this place, it is known as "The Hell of Tears." *A.k.a." The trail of tears."* Demons pretend to be Native Americans forcing the wandering souls into the pit of hellfire, near the River Bile. They wail and scream as they fall and the demons kick and strike them making them stand, shoving them into the pits of hellfire. As our warriors get closer to the River Bile, they are shocked to see to massive transatlantic slave ships of 1619. Tied to the masts are humans that decorate the décor as if they were a silver tinsel string that adorns Christmas trees. They scream out "Forgive me" as the ships crash into large waves of bile and their bodies bathed in its rancid fluids over and over eternal. Does it seem impossible for large waves and huge ships? In hell, the normal laws of man do not apply, for here torture is the meal of the day. Sadly to say these demons specialize in it, with huge insatiable appetites.

Closer they get as they traverse the surface and witness astonishing, and terrible sights that permeate the land. They come across several bodies being pulled further down into hell by many clawed misshaped hands. The faces of those become fully recognizable; it is Sazim and his broken "Paradox of Pain". He notices Warcast as he tries to pull himself against the powerful clutches of evil, that insist that he gets what is truly deserved by him and his followers. He thought that this was his ultimate call to duty, as he calls out to Warcast begging for help.

"I beseech you, surely you will not allow me to perish this way. You call yourself righteous, noble what about you is noble if you allow me to perish this way?

HELP ME DAMN YOU!" Sazim screams.

His words cut at Warcast as he ponders what to do next. The good in him has produced conflict with hearing the words of Sazim.

"You better keep moving, he is here because of what he helped unleash. So are all the stupid humans that are here with him, everyone, everywhere, all the way down to microbes, in every dimension is finished because of the stupidity of your humans." Bish bah says.

"Yes let him and all with him be punished for what they did to Cobalt, but how is it that the witch Vesha is not here amongst the damned. She should most assuredly be present." Outrage adds.

"This man's fate is different, he is merely being pulled down while the others are being slowly digested by the surface. Their bodies are being liquefied, truly dread." Cinder Hawk says.

Sazim continues to claw at the flesh-like surface as he is being pulled down, below the surface one of his legs is ripped off and he screams. The scream pulls at the humanity of Warcast, as he is tempted to help him. His elfin half says no, and his human side forces him to make a terrible error in judgment. He rushes forward and grabs the arm of Sazim trying to pull him from his fate.

"I know that you would have simply just passed me by as if I were nothing, I am not you, I am one of the seven we save every life when can no matter how defiled it may be!" Warcast says.

"WHAT HAVE YOU DONE, YOU HAVE JUST INTERFERED IN THE PUNISHMENT FROM THE DIVINE. YOU HAVE UNLEASED THE GENERALS OF HELL, AND HE IS LEGION YOU FOOL. I TOLD YOU NOT TO GET INVOLVED, PREPARE FOR THE

DAMNED I DIDN'T BELIEVE YOU WOULD BE THIS STUPID!" Bish bah yells, for now, they come evil and unstoppable.

"Pull you fool, lift yourself I can not do it for you!" Warcast says as he tries desperately to pull Sazim up!

"Look who's calling who a fool, I will hate you for my mother's sake. I will drag you with the last ounce of my strength. You will suffer with me forever, I will never let go of you, and I have added a binding spell that prevents me from releasing you. JOIN ME IN MY PERSONAL HELL BASTARD!" Sazim screams, and it is true Warcast cannot break his grasp.

The delirious laughter of Sazim becomes more out of control, and energy crackles around them. Suddenly an ominous greyish white hole opens in the sky, the wind picks up as lightning begins to strike the surface. All of the demons stop their infamous careers of torture as parts of the forest freeze over. Footprints begin to move towards the crew, but the maker of the footprints that crack the icy surface remains unseen. Invisible still the demons all make a path, allowing this new threat to move closer. Sazim begins to pull Warcast down with him when Bish bah makes a bold move. He flies so fast that he severs the hand of Sazim, freeing Warcast; with this, the hands stick fingers into his mouth, and his eyes, which are now filled with terror. His journey into hell is complete his ultimate punishment for help starting at the end of all. Sazim screams echo throughout the land, and then silence he has been dragged into his hell.

"I told you not to interfere, have just made this a very difficult mission now. You have just unleashed the one known in life as "H.H. Holmes the Harvester" the demonic embodiment of pure hate. He is America's first serial killer back in 1890; his pain is legendary, and only hell can hold his hate. As if we needed this tougher, you should know better, I expected this from the big blue whatever he is but you. That invisible force making those prints is him his evil is unmistakable, let's just hope that's all your thoughtless stupidity has awakened!" Bish bah explains

"Let him come, let them all come crushing them will be all the more pleasant for I grow weary of this place let us dispatch them quickly. Retrieve our objective and take leave!" Outrage says as he begins to clutch his golden mystic hammer preparing for the impending battle.

"Harvester" has taken form and the demons join him, he has white tattered pants and is shirtless. Faces of the evilest hatemongers our world has known move all over his body trying to escape his skin the faces of Hitler, Pontius Pilate, and White supremacy leaders are clearly in unrelenting pain and torment. They are moving all over his body trying to find a spot to escape the hell they created for themselves when they were amongst the living. The surface of his skin is alive like living tattoos, fluids leak from his body until the demons cover him with a tattered trench coat and ragged hat. He has no face as the damned souls course over his faceless head and body, he completes his outfit with a large white hat that resembles those that are worn by the Amish. He then points to our warriors with a smoking icy finger, as dozens of demons run towards our heroes. His head vibrates left to right becoming a blur, under his broad brim hat!

"Well if this is how I must go then so be it!" Cinder Hawk says as he draws a bow accompanied with iron-tipped blessed arrows.

"Well I ain't dying down here they are about to feel why my race is feared everywhere!" Bish bah adds.

"My friends I am truly sorry, I was foolish in my decision, I will not give in to such folly again!" Warcast replies.

Outrage yells in a tone that sounds like a thousand Lions, the rest add to the acoustic barrage. They charge forward crashing into the demons, Bish bah unleashes sickles of energy cutting first then punching through each opening made with blistering speed. His attack causes the demons to explode with divine light breaking through every eye, nose, mouth, and cut of each demon he strikes! Demons try to group assault Outrage only to find that he is at peak power, as his hand clutches the throat of a demon. He then brings his hammer down on top of the head still in his hand, splattering it into a yellowish-brown paste. Outrage then jumps and lands crushing about five more demons, yelling in the delight of battle as he crushes the beasts beneath his feet.

Now it is time for Cinder Hawk, as more demonic creatures crawl out of the trees. They attempt to flank Outrage, but the reflexes of Cinder Hawks bow bring that assault to a screeching halt. He fires multiple iron-tipped arrows into the back, head, and chest of the demonic assailants. Iron being one of the earth-based catalysts for all supernatural forces has caused an allergic reaction to the demons causing them to writhe in pain, before disintegrating into glowing particles.

Warcast angry from his prior misjudgment, conjurors up hundreds of silver and iron five-inch diameter ball bearing. They hover in front of his face and then they are fired into the attacking hell-spawned horde. The ball bearings rip through the demons like wet paper, and the impact sound is like bubble tape as they are struck. Their demonic fluids are splattered around the flesh-covered surface, which angers Harvester. More demons join the fray as they attack without fear looking for more successful ways to ambush the warriors. Cinder Hawk has his bow knocked from his hands; the demon takes delight in this minor victory. He makes a mistake and reaches for Cinder, Cinder quickly removes both hands of the demon with two blessed razor-sharp iron tomahawks that were tucked in the small of his back. The demon is no longer amused as Bish bah finishes him off with a blast of divine energy. All that is left of the demon are its probing eyes that roll across the ground. The fight heats up as they force the demons back, but Harvester's head still shaking back and forth violently in an obscure blur moves his coat back. He exposes his mosaic hate-faced body and lifts his hands to the energy opening in the sky above. He seems to be trying to bring forward something, something evil one would suspect. Warcast then hits Harvester with a powerful energy blast that staggers him back, smoldering from the blast demons gather providing a barricade to protect him from further harm. They are obliterated outright, as Outrage smashes the blockade and smacks Harvester in the head knocking him to his knees. They must end this battle quickly; the area that has what they are seeking has begun to glow.

"This battle is over hellspawn, but I wish it not to be my hammer needs more heads to ring and I hope that's the reason you keep lifting your foolish hands, you wish to volunteer?" Outrage taunts as the others continue the fight.

Cinder Hawk attacks two more demons; with one swipe he removes a demonic leg then spins and removes the other leg just above the kneecap. The other demon tries to assist but is savagely met with a tomahawk cleaving its head down the middle. The demon falls to the ground on both knees as he turns into a flaming vapor. He notices a demon trying to run from battle, Cinder Hawk hurls one of his tomahawks catching between its boney shoulder blades, it shrieks in pain and is reduced to nothingness. Cinder Hawk then retrieves his potent weapon from the surface as more demons march forward. Warcast then sends Gail force winds, hurling back the demons, and then Bash bah ends the scurrying evil with a shockwave of power that fries all in the path of the blast. They run back into the forest, all save one… Harvester. Harvester grabs his hat from the ground, which was knocked off and places it on his head, and raises his hands the sky is filled with red lightning followed by rain that is sapping weakening the warriors they can barely stand.

"Gotta stop him he will claim us all, we can't go out like this? 'Bish bah says.

"To the contrary, you will go out, exactly like that utterly painfully. Clearly, this is your end and I will gladly and your souls to my body for eternity. Let my lesson to your every lasting Hell begin!" Harvester says in a raspy sinister voice.

"This is unholy blood rain from the evil that men do close your eyes do not speak, it will enter your bodies quicker and then lay claim to your souls!" Warcast replies as he tries to come up with a plan to stop the general of hell!

L.A. Kendrick

Chapter 3

"Blood Rain"

With only one chance, Warcast calls upon a mystic force field of pure light, which is reinforced by Bish bah's divine energy. They all regain slowly regain their strength the rain can no longer touch them. Warcast then casts a spell to remove any demonic impurities the blood rain has caused, but the rain has not stopped. Something is happening to the sky portal opened by Harvester, thunder is deafening as a red tornado streaks down. It begins ripping up the Forest of the fallen flesh, all demons and the living hell trees are being sucked up into its vortex. The strange dark shadows and creatures that float in the sky are also vacuumed into the powerful opening. Debris impales the body of Harvester, he simply pulls the projectiles from his body. As quickly as the tornadic force touches down it leaves with the same speed. Harvester looks upward as do the heroes, a ball of green and black fire shoots from the opening in the sky. It strikes the surface hard, and the flesh-covered surface is scorched. Bish bah has seen this before as the fireball begins to take form.

"We need to leave, now fast that thing that just landed is beyond any foe you have ever faced!" Bish bah says as he is clearly disturbed as he looks at Warcast and closes his eyes while releasing a long sigh.

"Bish bah what is this thing, I take it you have seen this before. You look a bit shaken, I've never seen you shaken ever?" Cinder Hawk asks.

"What we have here, thanks to Warcast is not only the releasing of one the most powerful generals of hell. He has opened a gate into Purgatory, that thing is the part of the oldest race of our dimension. Older than angels and demons both, it was said that GOD ordered Archangels, Michael, Uriel, and Metatron to seal them away in the newly formed prison, Purgatory. They are more powerful than both demons and most angels only a handful of angels are more powerful. That my friend is Trenogog king of the Leviathans, he will lay waste to all to reclaim his place in our world we need to move!" Bish bah says calmly as Trenogog takes form.

Trenogog is grayish in color with the body of a great ape, hair hanging from the forearms, and legs from the patella down. With four-fingered clawed hands attached to four arms and four-toed legs. The head was covered in a huge black lions-styled mane, eyes of a great owl black and lifeless, void of a nose, with a chin, protruding with wormlike tentacles. Then a huge shark mouth with rows of teeth is slowly formed as it is adapting to once again being in our dimension after billions of years. His mouth is wide open as he drinks the demonic blood rain as if growing stronger. Harvester seems frightened by the sight, for he knows what is to come. Leviathans have unquenchable hunger; they will eat anything, humans, demons, angels, and even each other. They are notoriously hard to kill, which makes them exceptionally formidable, but hell has a way to kill anything, well almost anything.

The demons start scurrying, while some attack, but the ones that attacked are smashed and devoured whole. Trenogog has grown to a staggering twenty feet; his adaptation to our world is complete. He now has his sights set on Harvester, and now their battle ensues. Trenogog charges Harvester and is met with his bladed hat across his eyes. Harvester then turns to attack our heroes; he tries to cut through the force field that has been protecting them from the blood rain. Warcast makes an opening in the barrier so that Outrage can deal with him. Outrage grabs Harvester by the throat and forces him back, Cinder Hawk opens up with a spread of divine arrows into the face-covered body of Harvester. He is weakened by the assault when he is then met with a powerful blast from Bish bah that sends him flying yards backward skipping across the surface. As he tries to regain his senses and procure his hat embedded in a demonic tree. He is met with a low growl, as he turns to look he is snatched up by a mighty hand that belongs to Trenogog. He is about to be eaten as he fights back with all he has, still in the grip of the ancient beast he is punched into the surface repeatedly. Trenogog then opens his mouth to insert Harvester, as he tries to bite down Harvester still very strong, holds the jaws open.

"Let's go while he has something in his teeth, over there is where the crossroad demons make their deals across dimensions. The centerpiece is what we gotta get to!" Bish bah says as the demons pursue them and Warcast shield becomes weaker from the demonic evil shower.

They push forward as Warcast has one last parting gift for Harvester. He hurls a powerful mystic ball of light striking him. The jaws of Trenogog slam shut as he begins to chew and savor his hellish treat he then spits out Harvester's hat. With this, he releases a tremendous roar and slowly starts to pursue the warriors.

"Warcast you must stop this blood rain we will not make it if you don't it taxes our very life force. I will attempt to purify the blood rain with a spiritual rain dance, but I will need your help ready yourself!" Cinder Hawk says as he begins his holy rain dance passed on by his ancestors.

The rain has lightened in color but it is not enough. Warcast then releases his barrier and fires lightning into the darkened sky. The rain has become clear and has been turned into holy water. The demons are burned and scream as their unholy bodies are tortured by the powerful downpour of holy water they begin to perish. Trenogog feels great pain also as he picks up his pace to stop them. The surface becomes covered with the pasty dissolved remains of the dead or dying demons, making it difficult for the behemoth to pursue faster.

As the purified holy rain washes off the demonic blood rain from the bodies of the warriors, Outrage turns to do battle, he is of the royal guard and will not run from battle no matter how dangerous. The blood rain is washed down to where he can see it pool beneath his feet he comes to a decision. He has Trenogog in his cross-hair; the thrill of battle and completion of the mission overtakes him.

"Without trying to sound like a scene from one of the many action earth movies, I need you all to go and get what we came for. I'm positive that I can hold him here, but I will have to unleash my full wrath on him. This might pose a problem because I will release havoc on this creature and you might be washed in the wake of the pain I will cause!" Outrage says.

"Listen to you big blue whatever you are, that thing ain't like what you are used to fighting this is a being that is older than most of the universe. It's been killing loud mouths like you before you were a hope, even angels no less. Or didn't you hear that part, he is clearly outta your league GOD's soldiers? We either do this as a team and move or it will kill us all it's that simple." Bish bah replies, but Outrage does not listen!

Outrage charges Trenogog when they are only a football throw to the bridge leading to their spoils. He crushes through the demons that are trying to flee forward and past the devouring Trenogog. Outrage leaps high and lands hard on the back of Trenogog as the monster tries to grab him. Repeatedly he slams his hammer down over and over on the skull of the beast. In pain Trenogog slaps Outrage from his head and stomps him, to his amazement Outrage pushes his foot off knocking him off balance. Demons half dissolved by the holy rain, begin to attack Outrage, and this is too much for the others as they turn and join the battle once more. Warcast sends hardened salt shards flying into the bodies of the demons stunning them. As the holy rain finishes them off, Trenogog reaches for Outrage, but quickly finds a powerful Bish bah punching through his eye and out the back of his skull explosively. Bellowing in pain, and grabbing the eye, Outrage takes a mighty swing and knocks the staggering Leviathan off his feet.

"This is our moment he is down, just a little further over there. Let us waste no more time!" Cinder Hawk says as they move to the bridge of crossroads, but Trenogog has a secret that his kind shares regeneration.

Trenogog even half blind and holding his eye staggers to his feet and blindly pursues them based on sound alone. He gradually catches up to them and they fight once more. Cinder Hawk fires the special arrows into the flesh of Trenogog, Warcast summons lightning that strikes the many iron arrows embedded in his body. The shock has the jolt of ten billion watts, but Trenogog is only for the moment moderately phased. They press on almost to the crossroad and its promising jewel and only means of escape. Trenogog slaps the ground staggering the warriors, Outrage whacks his huge hand with his hammer enchanted. Trenogog pulls back and begins to hurl boulders with other debris that is readily available. Most are destroyed while still airborne by the lightning that Warcast has unleashed, as well as being crushed by Outrages hammer and Bish bah's divine energy blasts.

"For my ridiculous part in his being here I will finish him, the rest of you get across the bridge I have a plan. Outrage you need to strike the surface, the entirety of your run to the bridge I have a plan for our dear Trenogog. Make it so my friend and take your leave post haste!" Warcast requests, as demonic bats, attack Trenogog slashing and biting at his face, body, and eyes. He snatches and consumes, many of them, in the fray Warcast, and the others take to the path of the bridge.

The rain has stopped leaving the surface cleansed and saturated but the powerful strikes caused by Outrage have left many destabilized holes. Trenogog rushes forward unaware that Warcast has laid a camouflage surface over each. He falls knee-deep into them one after the other. The demon bats continue to attack him fiercely, he releases white flames from his mouth transforming them into ice. They fall crashing to the ground shattering upon impact. As they reach the bridge, Warcast slips past Trenogog, he yells to the other to press on.

"Now Trenogog we end this battle, I'm going to send you back to the ancient pit that you deserve. Now face me if you dare because I so dare to face you in battle for I am a descendant of The Light Lords' walkers of light!" Warcast yells, as Trenogog turns to face him there is only a smirk on the face of Trenogog and then a half-smile becomes a menacing frown. Warcast stuns him with purified light bursts, as conjures blades of the same divine light source to fly cutting the body of Trenogog. There is an opening between the legs of the great beast, Warcast makes his planned move; he runs sliding through the opening that his spaced legs have provided. As he slides on his side magically he drags the remaining holy water from their surface with him. It covers the surface of approximately ten feet on the bridge, as Trenogog releases his flaming icy breath. He tries to engulf Warcast but he is too fast for the monster, his unholy flame exposes each remaining trap. Trenogog cackles, leaping past the traps still airborne he fires his flames. Staggering Warcast back on the bridge, knocking him from the bridge Warcast can see the dark Lair of Lucifer below him as he hangs on for dear life.

Trenogog begins to make his move to kill Warcast; each step shakes the bridge violently making it difficult for Warcast to regain his footing. He climbs up scooting back from the giant Leviathan, pushing back hard with hands and feet placing distance between the two.

"There will be no reward of death for you this day monster, stand fast or I shall cut you down vile creature. YOU WILL ADVANCE NO FURTHER!" Warcast says as he looks over the edge into the great abyss of darkness and, frost-riddled winds.

Trenogog charges forward not realizing that he has frozen the bridge, and the holy water that was pooled across the bridge is now slippery and frozen Warcast has made it fragile. Warcast again strikes with lightning to the eyes as Trenogog is blinded he slips and falls crashing the bridge at its weak point. As he falls downward he catches his neck on the broken sharp bridge's edges, nearly decapitating him. Trenogog falls to his end in what seems like an eternal plunge, for him the next stop is the Lair of Lucifer. All that can be heard are the bellows of the creature as the darkness of the abyss claims him. Warcast then joins the others at the crossroads intersection as they make a startling revelation.

"There is nothing here, all of this for what, WHAT!" Outrage says

"Calm your big blue whatever you are down, Warcast if you please!" Bish bah replies.

Warcast uses a spell of truth, which exposes the hidden ruined building the crossroad demons use to make deals with mortals. They enter and the foe is none other than the horseman ROT hovering over the body of none other than their fallen comrade Cobalt. In his right-hand ROT has the soul of Cobalt he has claimed it from Horus. He looks very old, but also very powerful. Hairless gray and wrinkled he places one hand under his chin as if studying lab animals. Rot tilts his head to one side then sighs.

"RELEASE HIM, YOU HAVE NO CLAIM ON HIM IT WAS NOT HIS TIME AND THIS YOU KNOW, HAVE YOU NO HONOR?" Outrage yells.

"I am beyond good, evil, honor, dishonor you would be wise to lower your tone unless you wish to be one with your friend mortal!" Rot responds

"I challenge you for his soul, let us begin!" Outrage replies.

"I'm going to regret this, but we challenge you for his soul!" Bish bah adds.

They stand ready to do battle; this is what makes certain mortals different, the willingness to lay down their lives for one another. Had there been more like these four perhaps the Rapture would have been delayed a while longer. But as it stands much of the world is in flames man has lost his way.

"You mortals are curious, to say the least, you would be willing to lay down your lives for one soul. The only thing is that it is not your time; the highest power has plans that include the lot of you. So I decree that this is not yet your time. For your selfless, act I will place his soul back into his body, but only one of you will leave, the others will ascend to the next plane of existence. One of you will remain a witness to the destruction, pain, and agony of all. I will have more than enough to satisfy my job description when this has all passed." Rot says as he waves his skinny hand over the body of Cobalt his life force rejoins his once empty shell. Then there is the sound of a heartbeat our young hero lives!

"Man that was some dream, I dreamed I was dead why are you guys looking at me like that?" Cobalt asks as Outrage and Warcast embrace him.

"I would like to thank you for coming to Hell and tracking down our friend, I will always be in your debt." Outrage says as he extends his hand to Cinder Hawk and Bish bah.

"Well, you big blue whatever you are, you are welcome but I feel that our time is up I hope this was worth the trip here. You bums will always have a part of your souls tainted by this place. The creator is calling me and Cinder Hawk home." Bish bah replies as he and Cinder Hawk shake their hands.

"I do not envy what you have left to do here on earth, but it was an honor like no other to battle with you!" Cinder Hawk says, and in the time it takes eyelids to meet they are gone.

"What did I miss you guys?" Cobalt asks.

"I will tell you later, now climb off that table and let's go home!" Warcast says

"As I said before only one will be allowed to go, this is the Rapture. I have reaped Lucifer and this place will be destroyed it's minions have mostly entered the surface plane to your dimension. They are helping destroy your world!" Rot adds

"Is there nothing we can do to stop this, can we not have a second chance to redeem ourselves we can change?" Warcast asks

"This is beyond my proverbial pay scale, he has grown tired of your existence mercy was shown over and over again. All things have their limits!" Rot says as he grabs his tattered robe and places it over his shoulder.

"So what of my friends?" Warcast asks

"What friends?" Rot replies as Warcast turn to his friends they are gone.

"Now what is my fate?" Warcast says with fear in his heart.

"I will send you back to your world, your plan has worked, but the others will not be as kind as I have been this hour. Take that path of light now I must destroy this most unclean of living quarters!" Rot replies as pulls out of the air a huge Scythe; he begins dismantling the whole of hell. Souls buy what seems to be millions fall from the sky, and into the dark void below screaming to their final eternal. Warcast escapes but as he does he can hear an enormous explosion, as all goes black.

"These humans are quite, strange they show much promise, it is of little surprise as to why the creator had so much faith in them. It is a shame that it has to come to this horrible end, they only want what they want, but there are a few that still believe that even at the end of all there is salvation. Still, they fight hoping to bring about some small chance, even though this world is most assuredly condemned. These Celestials are fascinating. Of all the life forces that I have met in the cosmos, I will have to say that you are the most deceptive. Even if you knew your day would come, why you would challenge forces that you cannot fathom is beyond reasoning. Nevertheless, I applaud you, for you have brought many civilizations to ruin, simply by channeling their egos. Here it has been said that "The greatest trick the devil has ever played on mankind is making mankind believe that he does not exist". I say unto you BRAVO, for then you were able to bring these mortals to ruin. There, there is no need to throw a tantrum, all bad children deserve a spanking and you are long over due!" Rot says as he floats in the dark void that was once hell, but then he pulls an orb of light out of the darkness. It contains Lucifer who will be taken for punishment as he pounds against the wall of the orb. Rot smiles at him while pondering the end of all, for him business is good!

50

Chapter 4

"Combaticus"

A.k.a. War

New Orleans Louisiana, Mardi Gras time, Relick and Shabazz have just left Shreveport where they acquired a tip from a gentleman called Big O. They have been tracking the horseman Combaticus A.K.A. War, Big O has told them about the strange actions of people fighting world wide but told them that the violence and agitation seem extremely high here since Mardi Gras has started. One would expect no less given that the apocalypse has begun, most cities are either in ruins, over run by demons, dying from unexplained seemingly supernatural diseases, or overwhelmed by starvation. The Celestial Seven have split into separate teams to try and quell the unstoppable situation, but the key word is trying because it seems as though the war has found them here in the Big Easy!

"Big O seemed to be right on the money, I can feel the tension here, the funny thing is that horseman isn't the only thing here. There is something else here very powerful, and very strong. The gem of destiny has never buzzed so violently since this whole thing started!"

Relick says as he stops the car so that he and Shabazz can confront the root of the problem. They sit in the car watching the people shouting, and running in the streets a good time is being had by all it would seem.

"I know they do this to hide their fear by burying this situation in the only way they know how. In familiar good times, but you would think that they would be somewhere reflecting on what has brought this about. Shabazz replies as the night sky is filled with explosions and cheers.

"When do people ever do what you expect? It's like its part of our make up to do the unorthodox. I keep trying to understand why, we use to challenge ourselves more, you know to be tougher or stronger with this demon in the white house, and the so-called sane Americans voted him in. Now that's just a thing of the past, what am I saying none of that matters anymore!" Relick says as he looks down and then out through the driver's side window.

Suddenly his cell phone starts vibrating he is getting a call from Warcast with very important news.

"Whatcha got for me, we are down in New Orleans please give me some good news?" Relick asks as he places his cell phone on speaker for Shabazz to hear also.

"Well, Hell is like no other place you can imagine and a place that I never wish to venture to again. Our goals however were met, as several lost their lives in that place. Relick we found Cobalt the entity Rot had him, but for some bizarre reason had his body and soul as he presided over him. He then placed Cobalt's soul back into his body. Bringing him back to life, however, he does not remember much!" Warcast says.

"Ok, so where is Cobalt let me speak to em, he owes me a video game battle?" Relick asks as he anticipates speaking to his friend.

"Alas, I was the only one of my crew allowed to return to our world, before my eyes Outrage, Cobalt, Cinder Hawk, and Bish bah vanished. Rot claimed that they would no longer be part of this battle. As he said the Rapture would take many and leave others to bear witness to the end of all!"

Stunned for a moment, Relicks is saddened for a moment, he then gathers his resolve and focuses on the current mission maybe he can still right things.

"Did putting him back change anything, you know as Horus suggested?" Relick asks.

"I believe so, by restoring him I believe that it has weakened the Horsemen. Part of the prophecy has been broken, but not enough on the level of stopping this outright. So their strength has been diminished somewhat, but an unknown heavy hitter is here, and according to Rot will be unaffected by our gambit. He will end us all,

Rot seemed not to challenge us for the soul of Cobalt as if he were trying to aide us in some way!" Warcast replies.

"We have to try something stopping the Horsemen, getting rid of the demons might just turn the tide or something. It's just not in my nature to not try!" Relick says as he tries to locate a bright spot here at the end of all things.

"Let it be known that there is a concentrated evil at the exact location at which you are present. It's one of the last locations of evil, that still remains on earth a great deal of blood was spilled in that state in its infancy. Unrest with souls would be teeming to get revenge of some kind!" Warcast adds.

"This is nuts, man I would even go so far as to call this crazy. The hearts of man can get jacked up so easily. The world just seems to burn everywhere; all of our science is useless. I won't give up on my faith, we have to believe now more than ever!" Relick says as Shabazz looks on cool and steady as ever.

"I shall endeavor to keep you informed, but for now allow me to do further research. Oh, remember the battle at Stonehenge"? Warcast asks.

"Yeah, ok what about it?" Relick asks.

"When I was whisked back into our reality I saw the head of the zombie creature Half-Hell that you severed. It was flying back with me, and I tried to locate it, but during the chaotic trip back I lost sight of it. For some reason, it seemed alive and angry its purpose I have no idea?" Warcast says.

"Damn, well one problem at a time, well truth be told it won't matter anyway if we don't come up with a stopping plan for Ragnorok. I'll call you once we find Combaticus, Relick out bro!"

The conversation ends Relick and Shabazz remain quite, until Shabazz notices a club across the street and then attempts to change the mood.

"We should go there, maybe what we seek is in there waiting for us? Oh, I almost forgot made some new improvements on your Holo-Googles, contact lens style more practical. That look is a bit played out, many have that style but they work the same way as your Goggles, holograms, and all!" Shabazz says.

"Thank you they look cool, oh great you got my eye color! Well maybe you're right about the whole club thing, let's do it!" Relick replies as they get out of the car and start for the club.

They push through the crowed street, as everybody seems to be having one last great time. Beads are being thrown all over women flashing breasts from under their shirts, some should have been arrested for the horror that they exposed under their shirts. Relick looks up at the night sky the moon is vaguely covered by clouds that allow the now constant full moon to peek out. Relick notices flashes of light around the moon and he narrows his eyes to make out what he is witnessing. Unable to come to any conclusion as to what the flashes may be, he turns and enters the club.

The door man checks his I.D. and cash allowing him to enter, Shabazz however being a beautiful lady is given free access, per the norm for most clubs. The club is jumping women are wearing gear of all styles, short skirts, tight jeans, tight pants, and fitting low-cut shirts to the delight of the men present. Shabazz and Relick take a seat at the bar on the look out for the horseman "Combaticus".

"I just know something's not right in this place, the vibe is all wrong can you feel it?" Relick asks Shabazz as he calls to the bartender.

"Nothing has been right for awhile now, all vibes everywhere are off, but I do see what you mean, and that demon you speak of in the White House is only doing what the gem of chaos knows resides in that sick vessel?" Shabazz says she sits probing the club seen.

"He's here but he's not the only one here can't really tell if he is good or evil. There is other stuff here that is evil though!" Relick replies as he frowns looking around the club.

"Well, I'm interested in this environment, never been to a club before. The dancing is cool, maybe a bit non-traditional but still amusing!" Shabazz says looking wide-eyed and smiling.

"I always thought it was a waste of time, occasionally you'll get a good dance, but if you are coming here looking for a relationship you can hang that up!" Relick responds folding his arms and leaning back on the stool trying to look cool.

"What do you mean by that!" Shabazz asks with one eyebrow raised.

"Think of it like this, this lifestyle generally stays with the regulars and is very hard to get out of the system. You meet the average joker here, thinking that you have a winner and you are in for a rude awakening. Cause they gonna be coming back here every chance they get and then try to make you believe that this is normal. Even once they call themselves committing to a relationship, this scene will call to them like cake to a fat kid!" Relick answers with a slight smirk.

"Seems as though you have given this a bit of thought, you must have left this part of your life out of our conversations?" Shabazz says.

"Gotta have some mystery to me, but look who is talking been with me my whole life and still know so very little about you," Relick responds.

"Bartender, can we get some drinks here? Order for me please I'm going to scout around this place maybe try these crude dancing steps!" Shabazz says as she leaves and gives an unexpected shout as she pushes through the dance floor.

"She is something else that's a beautiful woman if you don't mind me saying so." The Bartender says with his back turned to Relick.

"Yes she is, I mean she's definitely something else," Relick replies feeling a bit embarrassed by her ability to present the obvious by mere presence alone. For he too at times is smitten by her dazzling looks.

"My man what are you and the lady drinking, I take it she wanted you to pick out a drink for her?" The Bartender asks as he places both hands on the counter, with a towel over his right shoulder.

"Yeah let me get some cranberry easy ice, and get her ginger ale if you got it, wait in my drink add some club soda, please. While you're at it what's your name bro I'm Yorel?" Relick responds and asks.

"Maldonado, Roberto Maldonado Jr. You cats drinking light or just don't drink alcohol?" Maldonado questions.

"Yeah, taking our physical fitness seriously don't want to get caught slipping in a fight!" Relick replies rubbing his face.

"Well from the looks of it neither one of you need to worry about that, live a lil we are at the end of the world. Who could possibly be fighting any of this at the end of humankind?" Maldonado asks while setting Yorels drink down.

"There is always a fight going on if we want one or not. We fight against that monster that is human, primal, and just outright cruel. Somehow I just know we started this thing, I just know it and the universe has finally frowned on us!" Yorel says while taking a sip from his glass.

"So you believe we started this? I've been saying the same the build-up, the strange weather, wars, crazy, violence, disease, man it's even been said that those strange crop circles were warnings that no one either understood or didn't share the messages!" Maldonado replies.

"Man if you only knew, I believed that we could make a change, that somewhere if nowhere but in the smallest corner of our souls. That we would turn the corner and start looking out for each other like we were meant to do!" Yorel says.

"So what brings you here to the Big Easy? Surely you got family that you would like to be spending time with?" Maldonado asks.

"Those days of family seem long gone, you know how that can be. I and the young lady are here looking for someone or something. Heard you guys got a lot of crazy past your normal local crazy running around, basically, I guess one last adventure. What do they call it, a bucket list?" Yorel replies still slowly sipping on his drink.

"Oh no, man you don't want to go messing around with this stuff. These days here, are dark it's like a heavy evil has dropped on the world but down here like some extra junk has made this place it's home. Scares me to be out sometimes, but can't stay home and bury my head. These are the few places people seem to come to forget about what's going on in the world until…It's their time, I suppose I feel the same as they do?" Maldonado says as another man takes a seat at the bar, and he looks familiar to Yorel as the gem slightly pulses.

He recognizes the man…it is Drazor trying to conceal but mostly just trying to blend in his size and hair were a dead giveaway. Yorel will play it cool and not let Drazor know that he knows him.

"Hold on a minute Yorel let me help this man, what's it gonna be this evening friend?" Maldonado asks.

"Scotch on the rocks and keep 'em coming," Drazor replies in a raspy voice with fingers and hands interlocked.

"Pretty strong you trying to forget something friend?" Maldonado asks while setting up his drink.

"Listen I've got no time for small talk, and I'm not your friend just do your job!" Drazor replies with a very stern look.

"Ok, you got it!" Maldonado says slightly looking at Yorel.

"Well I don't envy your job dog, seems it can be very tough?" Yorel replies as Maldonado hands Drazor his drink.

"Can be, but especially with the end of the world looming everybody seems on edge. You and your lady friend don't seem to be rattled or bothered by it?" Maldonado says

"Gotta a lot of faith I feel I've lived a clean good life, should have a nice place when this is all done," Yorel replies as he keeps some of his attention on Drazor.

"Faith huh? Well, that's something I haven't heard anyone say here in a long time. It's like they've outgrown GOD or they just don't care. Now I'm not a preacher but I can sure tell you that given all the things that have led up to this point, the cause of this is lack of faith. For example, when you take prayer out of schools, don't allow parents to spank or discipline their own kids, you get chaos now it becomes not only the fall of the children, but the sins of the father become apparent!" Maldonado says.

"Yeah, but no one would have admitted this a year ago but now look at the world, they are trying to come up with every reason in the book to explain what is happening. If you look at it through the Sunday school lessons are not a joke they are legit, I mean like down to the letter word for word!" Yorel replies as Shabazz rejoins them.

"Got my drink?" Amire asks Aka Shabazz

"Oh yeah, the strongest Ginger ale in the house!" Yorel responds

"I've been looking over this place seems cool on the surface, but something is hiding here in plain sight that's the weird thing about it though. Just can not place what it is, I believe it is just the thing we are looking for?" Amire says.

Suddenly a guy comes up to the bar and starts putting his mack game down or so he thinks.

"Hey I've been watching you all night, and you must be in great shape cuz you've been running a marathon through my mind for the last hour and thirty minutes. May I please get you on the dance floor? That is if you are here alone? The club guy asks.

Now having never been asked by any other man to participate in any activities but Yorel. Shabazz is caught off guard and obviously flattered by his lame trivial rap game. Yorel is a bit shocked and frankly feeling for the first time since he's known her jealous. And Shabazz notices this and plays on this, after all, if this is the end she wants clear indications that Yorel Aka Relick has feelings, real feelings for her.

"Pretty weak approach, but yeah I'll dance with you lets go. Yorel watch my drink please?" Shabazz says with a sheepish grin on her face.

Yorel is speechless as a song by "L.S.G." titled "My Body pumps through the speakers and it is a very seductive number.

"Well for someone who is just a friend you sure seem moved by this moment!" Maldonado says slightly laughing.

"Nah you hallucinating, it's not like that between us!" Yorel answers as the music plays and Shabazz gives a sultry seductive dance.

As the lights strobe and illuminate the dance floor, all eyes become fixated on Shabazz. Her smooth moves mesmerize all the men in the club and infuriate all the women. She has been trained also in seductive dancing, but she has added a modern touch. She gazes at the man dancing with her, then at Yorel. Yorel quickly looks away inspired by her he can only look away for so long. He finds himself caught in the incredible wake that is Shabazz, he knew she was beautiful and sexy but never to this extent, her display is so exhilarating and so dynamic that he loses focus on the goal that they are here to achieve. She pop-locks shakes her moneymaker, and to kill them all the kiss of death yeah you guessed it the infamous TWERK! This is the show stopper so powerful is her performance, that the man that was brave enough to ask her to dance, faints literally on the dance floor. He is dragged off the dance floor, and the crowd is quiet then erupts in feverous applause. She then looks over her shoulder at Yorel and winks all this without even breaking a sweat!

"Man that girl is dope, I kid you not. If you got no emotions or feelings for her after that, then you are dead. I think she killed that dude that asked her to dance, they had to drag him off the floor!" Maldonado says while rubbing his head.

"Whew now that was fun, I don't get to cut loose like that often. Come to think of it I never have before what did you think?" Shabazz asks Yorel he clears his throat and then answers.

"That was really nice!" Yorel says

"Nice, nice that's it son? Sweetheart your drinks are on the house I've never seen anything like that, your boy on the dance floor is gonna need CPR!" Maldonado replies.

"Thank you so much, I'm gonna go freshen up in the lady's room let me take one more drink though!" Shabazz says as she notices Drazor and looks at Yorel he nods letting her know he's got it under control. She sets her glass down and makes her way through the still buzzing crowd on her way to the lady's room.

"Now back to our conversation, all the violence that's been happening nationwide is sad. I try not to think about it and keep it moving but, it hits home so hard that I don't have the will to move sometimes. These cops got me afraid to go home, get food, or gas all this new footage is for real. We've been talking about this for centuries the violence against blacks in America, this ain't nothing new, but so many people act like it is!" Maldonado says.

"The ones that cut me the deepest were the ones where the man in South Carolina was shot after he clearly posed no threat to the officer. He gunned that man down like he was a dog; it wasn't even a thought to shoot him he was running away. But get the part where he dropped

the Taser beside the guy's dead body to strengthen his story or…
Hell, I don't know what he was doing. The other was the brother in
N.Y.C on tape clearly saying over and over that he can't breathe, they
pressed on his head, neck, and back, and the illegal chokehold was
applied, they didn't even check his pulse or apply CPR. All on camera
at least one of the two was charged, I worry about my nieces,
nephews, and godchildren. I try to talk with them as often as I can
because this is an evil that lives in the hearts of men, this brought
about this crazy end we now see?" Yorel replies.

"Yeah, I can see your point, I'm glad I don't have any kids how
would I explain this?" Maldonado says as the man that was anti-
sociable opens up with a truth that is startling.

"You start by telling them the damn truth, you let them know the
harsh reality that the color of their skin makes them a target. That this
country cares more about homosexual rights and the stopping of
bullying over the senseless killing of black men….dogs, this country
gives dogs more rights than black people. A thing that has been going
on for over four hundred years, the gay thing is a choice in my
opinion but if you say that then the full punch of white liberals falls
on you like you have stepped into a prize fight, taking away your so-
called constitutional rights. Now, who's the bully or should I say the
new bullies? Every time a black person says that they are killing us
white America says shut up, you're lying no one's killing you, or my

favorite if you just corporate and act right then you won't get shot or killed. Tell that to the black man in South Carolina that was asked for his license by that cop, routine fucking traffic stop, the cop said then just started unloading a clip in him. Then the dumb ass cop had the nerve to say calm down! Drazor responds while trying to control his anger.

"I remember that he is being charged for that crime though, justice is sorta being served?" Yorel says as he is trying to assure himself that somehow this is true.

"WHAT, What the hell are you speaking are you some kinda Jim Crow, Willie Lynch recipient of the year boy? What justice are you talking about? We now have in this country somewhere around 900 plus hate groups. We are the only, the only such country with this problem, they don't give a damn about justice these muthafuckas see justice one way, for the white people, you, me, our Hispanic bartender we weren't a factor in the constitution of this country. They only want to control or destroy what they can't understand, they have the nerve to say this is one nation under GOD what god, the all mighty dollar cause that's it!" Drazor explodes in a verbal fit of rage and it's apparent that he is just getting started.

"He does have a strong point, I feel even though there are a lot of illegal Mexican immigrants. There are a bunch that came over and did this thing the right way, still, they lump us all into the same group!" Maldonado says seeming to be trying to find an answer in his mind!

"Ok, you still have to find the strength to rise above and make the right choices. Can't let 'em win, look at the shape of the world now. Does it really matter?" Relick responds.

"You do the history, you ain't neva saw where Anglos have been where they don't spread, death, hell, disease, rape, enslavement. This is not a fuckin fairytale this is hidden from American schools' cold hard facts, I had to learn this the hard way, they try to hide this reality that they created. Native Americans, then African Americans brought over in chains by the millions. You expect us to have a chance of understanding with them, yeah only when you don't have a hope, hell then they got you.

They say that racism doesn't exist, that it's betta then tell that to the Ex-Clippers owner, or the Atlanta Hawks general management and owners. We are…let me find the right term, a bunch of cash cows. Now if we talk about it then we are just angry how dare you call a group of oppressed people that have been held down for over four hundred years angry? NO GODDAMN IT, I HAVE RAGE, PLAIN AND SIMPLE. AFTER FOUR HUNDRED YEARS SHOULDN'T AMERICA BE TIRED, TIRED OF THEIR HATE, AND TIRED OF BEING IN DENIAL ABOUT THE FACT THAT THIS COUNTRY

WAS BORN WITH THE PATHOGEN HATE?" Drazor says while letting loose his anger.

"I know what you mean, I'm black too, and I wake up every day to the same nightmares over and over. This white cop killed this kid unarmed, this white cop shot this man, and these white cops severed this guy's spine and crushed his larynx. These cats… Most get off free while screaming I was in fear for my life, or are caught on tape trying to plant stuff on the bodies. But I keep trying… for the love of life I keep trying to make a difference and I won't stop until I do! Yorel replies with his frustration building, with each passing word in this quickly heated argument.

"That's it…Dog that's all you got? This end that we are facing I know what caused this, In Egypt, in 1980 a white man leading a so-called peaceful expedition lied, and took this gem of destiny, trying to take a gem of chaos. Despite the warnings, that's what they do in order to rule and have power over others. I'm angry and hate myself because of my skin color or the way I talk. I'm not the hypocrite running to get a fucking tan, or running around worshiping a white Jesus when the Bible clearly states that he was a or is a man of color so if you serve the white Jesus that means you support the Anti-Christ plain and simply you support a lie. Damn man, it's just crazy trying to wrap your head around this shit. Tell me I'm wrong. Stop me if I'm making this up, this country's history is deep hate without one real reason why it is at the core of their souls. Drazor asks while the other two become quiet looking at him and then at each other.

Yorel passes a twenty spot to the bartender asking for a refill when Drazor brings up another fact about the face on the twenty-dollar bill.

"Did you know your money, that twenty most native Americans won't touch it they will only take it in break downs of One's, Five's, Ten's to add up to that one bill which is the Twenty Dollar bill. Because of the one person on the damn thing, Andrew Jackson he broke the treaty forcing them from their land after they helped them survive the messed up cold winters, and win the war of 1812. What did they do give them smallpox-covered blankets, bacterial warfare, and force them at gunpoint down The Trail of Tears from their own land, fucked up ain't the word for it, don't get me started on what they did to us Black Wall Street 1921, Rose Wood 1923 wiped those towns of well to do blacks off the map where would we be today if they had left us alone? Black Wall Street was one of the most moneymaking cities in the nation hell the world at that time during the great depression. White America didn't want to integrate instead they chose to eradicate. The schoolbooks don't post that kinda sickness or hell, that's still being passed on today. Ask the average white person about these issues they do one or two things deny it or say they don't preach or teach hate. BULLSHIT somebody's teaching it, look at the colleges across what used to be our nation, the video posts by the white kids, get online and play a video game they are the first ones to start with the racist comments, hell the only ones I've seen once they realize that you are black. So who's teaching them the fool shit? I've heard it from Canada, and England, they ain't slick and don't get a pass, not once have I heard any of them say they cut out the racist shit but say something about gay, and man they clear the fuckin lobby! I mean it, man, our lives BLACK LIVES MATTER! Drazor says with a complete and utter passion that most would see as an angry black man.

The pain is felt as silence falls upon the two listeners, as they sit no answers come to their minds.

"I…don't know what to say, I can't deny the fact that I'm past sick of past and current horrors of America against blacks. What I will say though, is any white person that would be offended by this conversation shouldn't be because what you say is the truth based on fact. I would challenge them to change this perception or talk to their friends or family members to let go of hate. Don't see this as blacks taking shots at 'em, will that happen…all whites aren't like this but too many of them stand by and do nothing. This makes 'em very uncomfortable, but talking about it is the only way to change this just like we need to change some of our ways as black people. . So trust me when I say I know how you feel bro!" Yorel replies while looking into his glass swirling his drink around the ice cubes clinking against the walls of the glass.

But Drazor is about to explode in a fit of repressed rage and memories that even Yorel is unprepared for

"Change what they created this paranoia that black people have. Those jokers always say that when we kill, we are monsters, animals, or sick. But what about when they do this and more, they say aww they just need help, they can be rehabbed give 'em a chance, they have a mental issue and just need a lil therapy. Do you wonder why Mississippi, Alabama, parts of Texas, and a few other states have been just completely been wiped off the map? I believe with all the hate… that cosmic justice sought those bitches out first, gave 'em what they feel blacks don't deserve, JUSTICE!" Drazor replies.

"What are you talking about, man help me out here?" Yorel asks.

"THOSE FUCKIN MONSTERS RAPED, BEAT, AND MURDERED THE ONLY WOMAN I HAVE EVER, EVER LOVED. I DIDN'T STOP EM AT FIRST, THEY TRIED TO KILL ME AFTER THEY RAN US OFF THE ROAD, THEY BEAT ME WITH EVERYTHING IF I DIDN'T HAVE THESE ABILITIES, THEN THEY WOULD HAVE. THAT GANG OF WHITE SUPREMACY THUGS DIDN'T KNOW WHO THEY WERE FUCKIN WITH. THEN I HEARD HER SCREAM THOSE BASTARDS WERE ALL OVER HER LIKE MAGGOTS. I TORE INTO THOSE MUTHAFUCKERS; I RIPPED OUT HEARTS, EYES, TONGUES, THROATS, BALLS, ARMS, AND LEGS. Even remembered biting off my fingers. I

INFLICTED AS MUCH PAIN ON EM AS I COULD, KILLED EM ALL BUT TWO. As I went to finish those dirty bitches off, she called out to me, damn I should have chased them down like the dogs they were but I couldn't leave her not like that. I got closer to her, I closed my eyes for a second, she was a mess, so much blood my baby wasn't going to make it. I tried to stop the bleeding with my shirt, but she told me it was ok and that she wanted me to be the last thing she saw, she was so calm but her breathing was in short breaths. I called for help on my cell, but she died right in my arms, I held her as close as I could, like she was a second skin close. I don't remember when I stopped crying; I just recall the damn courtroom they let those punk sons of bitches off. I WAS NOT GONNA STAND FOR IT YOU KILL MY GIRL AND NOW YOU SIT HERE IN THIS COURTROOM LAUGHING AND GONNA GET OFF, I GRABBED ONE OF THE BITHCES AND THREW HIS PUNK ASS THREW A WALL. I KNOCKED THE OTHER ONE'S TEETH OUT AND BEGAN TO BEAT THE HELL OUTTA THAT MONSTER. THEY ALL PILED ON ME I THREW THEM OFF ME, THEN I WENT AFTER THE CROOKED JUDGE, SMASHED THE STAND, TURNED ON THE BAILIFFS, AND DESTROYED THE COURTROOM. THEN EVERYTHING WENT BLACK, I WOKE UP IN A JAIL CELL HOW'S THAT FOR YOUR GOTDAMNED JUSTICE IT FAILED ME...US SHE AIN'T COMING BACK SHE NEVER GOT JUSTICE I ONLY HOPED I KILLED EM ALL! I SUPPOSE THAT'S ALABAMA

JUSTICE, WITH THEIR SOUTH SHALL RISE AGAIN BULLSHIT! LET THAT REVERBERATE IN YOUR LIL HEADS FOR A WHILE!" Drazor says, the men are speechless, Yorel starts to wonder as he and Maldonado look in the direction of the seething Drazor.

"Well you guys are gonna really hate this, I just got this email to turn on the T.V. and it's pretty bad South Carolina!" Maldonado says as he turns on the T.V. above the bar.

(News reporter) Tragedy has just struck a church in South Carolina, a white male 21 yrs. Old sat in a historically black church for an hour. When he suddenly began firing shots from a high-caliber handgun, nine people were killed when the shooting stopped. He according to a witness said that he would allow her to live to tell the world what he did. He has been apprehended and he gave these chilling sadistic comments.

"I had to kill them, they rape our women, take all our jobs, and are taking over our country!"

(News reporter) End quote I just hope that justice is served to this monster, camera footage from the church help capture this crazed killer it is a sad day for our nation and the state of South Carolina we are far beyond the end times, amongst the slaughtered a state senator was killed which would imply a terroristic attack and a hate crime…In another breaking story, a white male in Las Vegas has gone on a killing spree, firing rounds into a concert crowd, injuring over 500 people, and the latest killing 56….

The T.V. is turned off and the three men are silent until Relick breaks that silence.

"Seems as though for four hundred years that thing that's under the bed or goes bump in the night. Blacks have a face to fit the monster, the white man. Some of them have helped us get to a certain point of peace but so many others are in denial about it…I just don't know what to say, it really doesn't matter now. Dr. Morgan with his quest for power has brought about the end of all things!" Yorel replies as he attempts to pay his tab, he can feel evil slipping into the room.

"That's it that's all you got!?! Really? You don't give two shits about black people our struggle you need to hear the rest of this you don't get to run away. He went into a church and killed innocent people on the hollowed ground, they were praying to God in these end times and this cracker bastard slaughtered them what do you say about that… HUH? I suggest you sit back down!" Drazor says as he grabs Yorel by the arm not allowing him to leave.

Yorel looks at his hand on his arm, then takes a deep breath and the last sip from his drink, and then addresses the issue of trying to hold him there.

"Bro…I don't know your pain for your girl and I tell you that I'm deeply sorry for what happened, but I'm only gonna tell you once about putting your hands on me! Yorel who is now becoming his alter ego RELICK as the building starts to shake.

"Or what sell out muthafucka, what the hell are you gonna do huh?" Drazor taunts a sword to his neck that is held in motion to meet his throat, courtesy of Shabazz.

"Or I shall make you a hole that we can see from Mars!" Shabazz says as Drazor looks at her slowly and the room stops shaking.

"Oh really you've picked the wrong cat to challenge I just wanted to make your boyfriend see the light, but if it's a knife fight you want…then it's a knife fight you'll get and you gonna find I'm a lot tougher to cut then that! You mighta heard of me they call me Drazor!" Drazor brags as he flicks his arms and two massive blades extend from his forearms like two switchblades.

"Yeah we know who you are, and we kicked the shit out of you and your team a while back. I understand she beat you all in a sandstorm like four on one. We ain't even gonna get started on what I did to your Paradox squad unless you need a repeat of pain?" Relick says as he holds Drazor's arm down on the counter top he is unable to budge. He is in shock because the words that have been spoken are true.

"Oh shit so what now, you are Relick and the infamous Shabazz? You could have ended this a long time ago. You could have forced white America to give us the respect, and justice we are due, and they promised. Stopped all these white supremacy groups any time they pop up. If I had your power, after what they did to my girl I'd be tossing white folk into space along with their fucking sheets with the eyes cut out. YOU COULD HAVE STOPPED ALL OF THIS! Drazor yells as he calms down realizing that he is clearly outmatched on either choice of the two.

Everyone close to them stops as if anticipating the fight and they begin to gather around. The room seems to take on a weird ambiance like the air is thicker and more sinister. Maldonado is shocked to be actually talking to Relick and Shabazz the whole time and didn't even notice. But there is an uneasy clapping at the counter by a muscular figure that makes them all give pause, all but Relick.

"Bravo, bravo doesn't take much to get you germs to fight or hate each other, if you're wondering who I am. They call me "Combaticus" a.k.a THE HORSEMAN OF WAR! And I'm afraid you are not the only ones searching for me I have been searching for you, and that sinister character at the far end of the bar would be "Set" who has killed his brother "Osiris" in order to acquire the "Gem of Chaos". He is totally hell-bent on conflict and death, which is right up the alley of "THE HORSEMEN OF WAR"

Chapter 5

Easy does not apply!

You seem to have this all figured out you hunt me, I hunt you, you fight me I kill you, things like that. Well let me thin the herd for you so we are not interrupted, the club is no longer jumping and well quite frankly they seem a bit scared!" With a simple head turn, Combaticus looks in the direction of the crowd too afraid to move and strange things start to happen on the dance floor.

Some simply evaporate, and some are being transformed but as for the reluctant witnesses to the end of all, they are frozen still. Those trying to take selfies are stuck in their picture-popping poses until Combaticus has his say.

"Ok, now we're where we, ah the end of all things, the ones that are not frozen we have another purpose for them. Now when I'm done talking we can do what we came to do you follow me?" Combaticus says as he swivels around on his bar stool.

"Not really sure why we gotta hear anything you gotta say chump, I say we jump you and let the janitor clean up the mess. Now that's a damn good thought?" Drazor replies as he stands ready to battle the evil that has gathered around them.

"I say we hear him out, see how deep this Mammoth Cave goes. Let's hear it Bozo!" Relick says.

"I'll make this really fast, since the fall of Adam and Eve mankind inherited the Chaos gene. The potential for you to destroy, and deceive, was magnified once this gene was added thanks to Lucifer. Each nationality, after the separation of the supercontinent Pangea carried it with them. While most were content with tribal wars, and conquering the local natives and wildlife, others were not. The domination of all drove them, and yes some cultures have a deeper desire to achieve this goal. All for some symbolic level of immortality!"

"The God complex, they would travel great distances to kill, steal, plunder, or whatever their dark souls desired. You can thank Cane for some of this, Satan had a particular passion for him, really he was patient zero, these psychologically challenged individuals carried not only the Chaos gene but are direct descendants of Cane's bloodline and we all know what he did to his very own brother. Attila the Hun, Alexander the Great, and Julius Caesar, just to touch on a few, had no moral compass just a desire to conquer. Oh, wait I've got to add that little short fellow, what was his name…Napoleon that's it. Then those who I like to call the "Sons of Cane" took to sea travel, tricking and taking from any that they encountered. They brought with them diseases that all but eradicated many civilizations, while screaming we come in peace raping and murdering women and children. That was the start of the end for you lower life forms I mean we just sat back and watched at how efficient you are at killing one another. War after war, our jobs became so easy, yes we did nudge you occasionally but the true nature of man always did the rest without much provocation. Here we are today, watching you still on the same path just like a pathogen metastasizing your way every place you've been. If we didn't do end it the aliens that you have captured surely would have laid waste to just this world, but what fun is that it would not have paid out in death tolls across everyting like you've done, for us you made buisness good, your kind do things on a grander scale, don't you? By other beings or races that have come into contact with you, they have been tainted with the chaos gene the human race carries, YOU HAVE ENDED THE COSMOS...FOOLS! YOU HAVE DONE SOME PRETTY IMPRESSIVE THINGS WITH MUSIC, ART, AND INVENTIONS BUT WHERE YOU REALLY EXCEL IS IN YOUR HATE, YOUR KILLING, AND YOUR DESIRE FOR WAR! (HE STANDS) ON THIS PLANET IT IS NOT MORE EVIDENT THAN RIGHT HERE IN AMERICA, YOU SAY YOU ARE THE LEADERS OF THE FREE WORLD, WRAPPED UP IN HIDDEN AGENDAS, AND POLITICS. ALWAYS WITH YOUR NOSES IN EVERY OTHER COUNTRY'S BUSINESS WHILE YOUR COUNTRY IMPLODES

FROM WITHIN, YOU SPARK MORE GLORIOUS CONFLICT BETWEEN THE REST OF THE WORLD. IT WAS SO EXHILARATING TO WITNESS, FOR ME AND MY KIND, I WAS BORN FOR THIS MAKE NO MISTAKE I AM ABOUT TO SHOW YOU WHY!" Combaticus says as he calls forth the army of the dead that came with the prophecy in Revelations.

"This is my world I hold the Gem of Chaos, I am the bringer of death, I will bring death to you Combaticus, and your God. This universe is mine!" Set says as he summons demons by slinging blood on the floor opening up portals to the surface of his pocket hell.

All that are in the club who were not already demons masquerading as humans have been tainted with the splashing blood of Set and stand ready to do battle. While the innocent ones simply vanish without a trace! Relick, Shabazz, and Drazor are surrounded for on one side they have Set and his growing demon horde, and on the other, they face Combaticus with his staggering zombie army. Relick is simply still sitting as Shabazz exposes her Nun chucks. Drazor however is showing symptoms of a man bent on destroying all his enemies.

"I don't give a damn about how this starts or ends, just give me something to cut. I think I'll start with you Set, I never liked you anyway?" Drazor says.

"Wait a minute you gonna have to choose sides this thing is bigger than you and we seem to be outnumbered team up or team with defeat. Somehow he has the "Gem of Chaos" Osiris had it and I don't see him here and I know he wouldn't give it up. How did you get it snake lips?" Relick asks still sitting calmly waiting for the battle to begin.

"I killed my weak brother for this, he was unworthy of wielding such power. Wanting you humans to worship us again, I just want to kill all of you and anything like Combaticus all of you make me sick ending you all will give me such pleasure. I am all the Horsemen pressed into one supreme being!" Set says as the gem glows bright and he pulls out his axes.

"Well that's exactly what snakes do, I guarantee you struck when he was not looking, coward?" Shabazz says as she stands ready for battle.

"SHABAZZ I WILL ENJOY PULLING YOUR SKELETON THROUGH YOUR SKIN. YOU WILL BE THE FIRST TO DIE BY MY NEWFOUND POWER! Don't think you get to leave here horseman I will add your power to mine also!" Set replies as he motions his death minions to battle.

"Way too much-talking snake lips, we've done this before and you know how this ends!" Shabazz says as she attacks.

She starts with a roundhouse kick knocking a demon over the counter smashing the huge mirror that outlooks the countertop. Maldonado covered in glass and alcohol escapes through the back door to safety. Other demons begin to rip into the humans left on the floor and in the building as the undead clan of Combaticus crash through windows trying to claim victims. Panic grips the crowd and they begin to stampede for the exit, knocking Shabazz to the ground Relick powered up and in disguise jumps to her aid parting the human herd like the Red Sea.

"You just gonna lay there all day or do something?" Relick asks jokingly

"So you got jokes, watch me now and learn a few things, bright boy!" Shabazz says as she attacks the demons and dead alike.

She activates mini projectile firing wall mounts she placed while she was giving the place a once over. They fire iron-blessed needles and pellets that penetrate some of the demons causing an allergic reaction. Upon entering the bodies of the unholy damned they begin bursting into blue and white flames, energy escapes from their eyes and mouths. Shabazz jumps in the air smacking a few demons on her airborne assault with her glowing nun chucks heads and other body parts exploding. As she lands on the top of the bar surface a demon grabs her and tries to throw her through a window. She quickly counters with blinding speed by wrapping the chain of her famous weapon around the creature's neck the force of momentum that the creature used against Shabazz is used against him. She uses the force to pull him clear over the counter surface while tightening the chain choke as it is illuminated by bluish energy she forces the head to pop off. The body of the demon begins to flop around on the ground only to be stilled by Shabazz punching through its back with a glove with a retractable iron blade on it. She then casually removes an eyeball from her nun chucks, which continues to move until she stomps it into a bloody yellow paste.

"Now this is what I'm talking about this ain't the work of surgery unless you have a Drazor blade! You like that huh, oh please believe me there is more and I intend to give you more!" Drazor says as he cuts demonic monsters and the dead that try to lay hands on him.

"You finally pick a side? Wise side to choose, you guys ready to WAR WITH ME?" Relick yells as he enters the ferocious fray.

"Now let's just see why he thinks you mortals are so special!?" Combaticus says as he streaks to intercept Relick.

The two warriors lock and punches are exchanged violently, Set has his eyes on an unsuspecting Shabazz. He seems to study her moves but to his amazement, she has an unorthodox fighting style that he cannot seem to match. And then the dead on the side of Combaticus begin to pound on the outside of the club some make their way inside.

A woman tries to run for the exit, but is pounced by a demon, she kicks and fights hard as the demon rips into her body the blood attracts a deadite. It staggers forward to her bleeding body they both are on her one trying to take her soul, the other consuming her body with each bite. She screams in utter pain as her leg is ripped from her body by the demon and he begins to beat her to death with it. Angry the demon smacks the deadite off his prey. Shabazz just smacks the demon, unable to save the woman as her Femoral artery squirts blood; she looks at Shabazz and then dies. Set seizes the moment because Shabazz is occupied he swings his axe sending a crimson blade intending to take her down. Relick notices this and jumps up planting both knees into the chin of Combaticus, Combaticus does a somersault flying out through a window and skipping across the surface. Relick in an eye blink grabs Shabazz shielding her from the shock blade of Set, but the force of impact is great and knocks them both out through the wall taking the entire side of the club with them. The momentum is stopped by a cargo van across the street.

"So does this make us even?" Relick says as he unfolds his arms that shield Shabazz from harm.

"Are you kidding you have to go way back for at least two decades to even come close, to how many times I've saved your spam!" Shabazz responds as she puts on faceplate-style armor. This is a first for her, which means that this is a battle for keeps. Combaticous then reveals a shocker to the dynamite duo, as he punches Relick sending him splitting multiple street lamps and bicycle stands.

"You are Shabazz I have watched you so long, the fire of combat, war, and carnage lives deep within you. And you don't embrace like a flirtatious schoolgirl being chased by all the popular guys. I know you won't be my hand of war so I recruited another and branded her. Endowing her with incredible might, to help end this, shall I bring her in?" Combaticus says as he motions for his new acolyte.

"You ain't the only one with an upgrade, how do you like me now because the Bitch is back?!" Vesha replies as she approaches with the mark of Combaticus on her forehead.

"You got that right, and I know the perfect kennel for Bitches!" Shabazz responds as Vesha is within a few feet.

Shabazz kicks Vesha in the face which would stop most any opponent in their tracks, but Vesha, this new version of Vesha is not having any of that as she is unaffected by it.

"Nice thump now it's my turn!" Vesha says as she grabs the shocked Shabazz by the leg and slings her down the street and through the windshield of a parked car.

Only her new body armor protected her, but she still felt most of the intended intent. Vesha begins to stalk her as she channels energy from the mark of Combaticus her hands begin to glow red. As she clutches her hands making a fist the air begins to crackle and the dust particles barely seen by the naked eye spark like fireflies around her fists. This is curious to Shabazz this is a method that even she is unfamiliar with.

"I am gonna take great pleasure in kicking your ass, this battle will prove who the best is, take this without a doubt!" Vesha replies as she leaps to the hood of the car that Shabazz is struggling to get free from.

Vesha strikes and Shabazz rolls out of the way of her fists. As Vesha punches through the hood of the car, Shabazz gives her a double kick in the face knocking her backward. Vesha is temporarily knocked off balance, tripping over a fire hydrant, giving Shabazz the time to distance herself from her. The streets begin to fill with the dead as they grab any would by innocent; they are soon accompanied by the demons of Set who only increase in the attack of the damned.

"People still continue to vanish in the blink of an eye, the prophecy is true!" Shabazz says as she slices the dead and damned alike with her powerful Noir Blade.

"Get off me dead things, when I cut her up you can have her parts to feast on, now get off me and allow me to ready your dinner!" Vesha says as she begins to dismantle the necro's barehanded punching through chests and skulls. Vesha's hands become covered with oily dead tissue, and she is enjoying this completely.

Suddenly there is a crash glass and debris fly toward Shabazz she blocks and deflects the building materials and glass. It all seems to be in slow motion, as Set has Drazor by the neck and slams him into the concrete with a monstrous thud.

"Mortal Bitch this what I do to traitors, but you…I will do far worst. For starters let me introduce you to my "Sizzlers" their touch is filled with chaos fire which will burn not only your flesh but your nasty soul!" Set says as he is still holding Drazor down with one hand, with the other he slams down his snake axe infused with the energy of the Chaos Gem, splitting the street five demons covered in flames crawl out ready to attack Shabazz. There is a problem because Vesha is closing the gap, but Shabazz being the ever-resourceful warrior has a backup plan.

"Stupid snake face did you think I didn't have an out, FIREBOLTZ show snake lips how we do it!" Shabazz replies as Tola, Rain, and Hera join the battle.

"We would have gotten here sooner, but you know traffic, the end of the world and all," Hera says ready with her bow staff.

"Just tell me what to cut!" Rain says with Sia's ready.

"I believe on the dotted lines?" Tola replies Tonfa's exposed.

"Vesha has turned to evil and has a new power she bears the mark of combat. She is even more dangerous than ever!" Shabazz replies.

"Still unstable and crazy as cat shit…Figures." Tola says

"I got her, been wanting to try her for the longest time," Hera replies as the two lock in combat.

"Oh Set watch your left!" Shabazz warns as Relick in a blue streak knocks him skipping through an armored transport.

"Man he stinks and talks too much let me finish this got to take one of these heavy hitters out of play!" Relick says but before he can go to finish Set, Combaticus swings a lamp pole. Relick catches it snatches it from his hands and begins to beat him with it until its rendered useless.

Relick kicks Combaticus in the chest dislodging his armor in that section. The dead come to aid their master, Relick then administers his brand of pain to the dead followers, he takes two cars and starts pounding his attackers into bloody stains. He slams one of the cars on top of the downed Combaticus so hard that a wheel is sent hurling into the dead and demons mowing them down.

Rain and Tola double-team the Sizzler demons; Rain strikes with multiple hits on the body of a flaming horror. It drops to its knees as Tola smacks it on the base of the neck severing the spinal cord. Rain then finishes it off by sticking both Sai into the sides of its skull. It burns in a flash; the body is reduced to a fine ash. A Sizzler runs scurrying the side of a building like a spider, thinking itself unseen. It attempts to pounce on Tola.

"TOLA LOOK OUT!" Rain screams as she with pinpoint accuracy throws one of her Sai's impaling the creature to the side of the building. It momentarily hangs from the building then it meets the same flaming reaction to their weapons.

"Good shot girl, told you that practice would pay off!" Tola replies, as she turns to thank Rain she is gone.

"RAIN…SHABAZZ RAIN IS GONE SHE WAS JUST HERE AND NOW SHE IS GONE!" Tola yells as Shabazz stops for a moment to try and explain quickly.

"Fear not she is gone to the next stage according to the Rapture, fear not for her we are the ones that will suffer through the hell that is to come!" Shabazz says while continuing to crave her name on the hordes of hell.

Shabazz turns to hear the battle between Vesha and Hera, Vesha is slightly gaining the upper hand. Shabazz leaps into the air digging her heels deep into the back of Vesha as Hera slaps Vesha across the face as she stumbles forward. For good measure, she thumps her in the stomach and shin. Vesha leans forward and Hera delivers a skull-crushing blow to the back of her head.

With this Vesha, catches Hera in the ribs with a stinging gut punch breaking a rib, she spits blood and begins to gasp for air. Shabazz becomes immersed in anger, and slices Vesha's upper thigh Vesha staggers back clutching her leg. She screams but it quickly turns into a blood-lust laugh. Shabazz runs to Hera to aid her.

"Can you continue the battle?" Shabazz asks as she signals to Tola as she kills the last Sizzler to help in the battle.

"I'm good let's get the bitch!" Hera replies.

"I DIDN'T COME FOR THESE SECOND STRING WHORES I CAME TO SEE THE FISTS OF DESTINY, MATCH THEM AGAINST ME!" Vesha screams as she attacks Shabazz.

With her fist glowing she punches Shabazz to the side of the head and repeatedly to her back Shabazz is hurt. Tola jumps in and brings the pain by peppering the head of Vesha over and over with her Tonfa's. Hera makes a bold move with her staff like an Olympic pole vaulted catches Vesha square in the chest with both feet and begins to bicycle kick her repeatedly in the chest and stomach until she losses momentum. Tola will not let up she also strikes like a keyboard operator until Vesha is driven back. Shabazz can recover thanks to her new uniform she was able to absorb most of the attack, although she still felt the barrage.

"Thank you, Lewis Lattimer, so glad I took the time to improve on my old tech!" Shabazz says to herself he was inspirational in the development of her love of science.

Mean while Set and Combaticus cut Relick off from the rest of the group, and the weird orb in the sky seems to get closer as Relick notices. He also notices how close air planes are flying by it seemingly not noticing the unusual anomaly.

"Your time now you no longer have a place in this thing that is to come!" Combaticus says.

"Yes, you will fall right here with the rest of these human maggots!" Set adds as he floats to his feet engulfed in crimson flames.

Relick looks around at the people screaming and running each time he tries to help them he is cut off by one of the two power's houses or their hordes.

"Well, that's funny because a snake is no more than an overgrown maggot in my book. You had to notice the similarities when you look in the mirror, even the short time before the mirror cracks under the weight of your nasty-looking face!" Relick replies and has become angrier at the damage he is unable to stop.

Nevertheless, he is determined to end this quickly as the two begin to debate on who is going to kill Relick first.

"I hold no alliance with anyone only my brothers, but we have tried to kill him as individuals and he so far has bested both of us. We can attack him at the same time while attacking each other in the process if it allows for it!" Comabticus says

"Yes agreed, but once he is done I will collect the gem from his corpse and deal with you and your God!"

A truce has been made; Combaticus is very cunning and looks to the sky at the bright star-like phenomena. Suddenly the two are caught in a battery of bullets and grenades then Combaticus is caught in the face with a high-speed manhole cover. Courtesy of Drazor as he cuts his way back into the battle, he has a few choice words.

"Too much damn talking it's the end of the world we don't have time for all the yang yang!" Drazor says as he cuts the face of Combaticus with his arm blades.

He only smiles as the cut slowly heals; he punches the ground jarring Drazor back a bit with the shock wave impact. Relick grabs Combaticus's bench presses him over his head and power-bombs him into the concrete sidewalk. Leaving and massive crack and a disoriented Combaticus, again Set tries his hand and attacks Relick along with Drazor.

Set begins to spew a corrosive acid that dissolves a street pole, a park bench, and two Jaguar cars. Relick knocks Drazor out of the way but not before some of the acids partially dissolve one of his metallic arm blades. The two warriors look at the steaming piles that use to be recognizable vehicles.

"Nice save, that was pretty close but those cars where nice, you gotta make a chump pay for doing that to such nice pieces of work!"

Drazor says as he pulls out two custom-made 44. Magnum handguns with armor piercing explosive tip rounds

He fires cutting down the dead, then focusing on Set and Combaticus he soon runs out of ammo and a bit of smoke remains hard to make out if they have had any effect on either of the two.

"You know that that's not gonna do it, I think they both are just a bit tougher than that?" Relick replies as he focuses on the area of smoke.

"I know I was saving them for you, sure as hell was fun shooting old snake face in the face though!"

Out of the slowly dissipating smoke, two forms begin to make way, accompanied by a screeching voice.

"Really going to love carving my name into your face, TRAITOR!" Set yells

"I believe he means you, I don't know him like that? 'Relicks says to Drazor

"Yep, it's me, didn't like him much bossy lil bastard. So you wanna rock paper scissors for who we wanna fight?" Drazor replies.

"Why not, even though I'm still just gonna pound on both of them until they stop twitching!" Relick says as they go through the motions of the game.

"Let's go Shabazz I don't have all day for this, you are going to die for all the humiliation that you've caused me all these years!" Vesha says.

"We are all here dumb ass and we all want a piece of you, you are just stupid a stupid lil pouty tramp!" Tola replies and takes it to Vesha hard.

Hera says nothing but attacks jabbing her bow staff in the face of Vesha then she swings her staff, and takes out her legs making her leave the ground for a moment. While Vesha is still airborne Hera brings her bow staff to the abdomen so hard and fast the air gives off a low hum, followed by a killer "WHACK" knocking the wind out of Vesha.

"You ain't talking so big now, let me go ahead and end this façade you call your revenge!" Tola says just as she is about to release the final blow, Tola vanishes the remaining three give pause for the moment.

Short-lived because Vesha explodes up in a fit of rage and attacks the two violently. She punches Hera in the stomach breaking a few ribs, but Hera continues to battle as if there is no damage. She flips over Vesha and lands behind her places her in a chokehold; Vesha then begins elbowing her in the stomach. Hera begins to cough blood, so she digs her fingers deep into the eyes of Vesha, but is then flipped off by her foe. With fists still glowing she punches the ground intending to crush the skull of Hera, but Shabazz pulls her out of the way just before the death blow. Vesha rubs and adjusts her eyes, and smiles at Shabazz tauntingly.

"Do you really think that if you did not have this additional, power that you would be able to deal with all of the Fire Boltz? I think not, you lack the discipline to be of any greatness, you want the Fists of Destiny? I'll give you just one, only because you have desecrated our clan, I assure you that I am going to beat you within an inch of your life. FOR THE TOMAS CLAN…LET'S DO THIS! Shabazz yells as Hera gathers herself to stand.

"This is what I came to see, PARTY TIME!" Vesha screams as the intensity glow of her fist have grown exponentially.

"Hera can you continue? If so lay back while I weaken her, the pride of Vesha will be her undoing. Shabazz says

"I can and will!" Hera replies

"YAHHHHHH!" Vesha screams as she runs at Shabazz.

Shabazz does not move but when Vesha gets within striking difference Shabazz simply side steps Vesha allowing her to sprint by only to be caught in the gut with a punch that make her spit puke. As she leans forward after the vomit has covered her mouth Shabazz flips in the air and while in mid-flight with legs spread like fingers promoting the peace sign. Kicks Vesha with one, or two strikes on the first leg punishing the right shoulder, other to the back of her brain. Vesha is no longer laughing or smiling she is only eating hard surfaces.

"You fight like we are still in school, we are not playing for stats we are playing for much higher stakes, now get your ass up!" Shabazz says uncharacteristically and hands motions for Vesha to continue the battle.

"Everything easy, everything in your favor, you were always the favorite, the one of chosen handed to you. I should be with him at his side crushing all that would stand before us. You have it all, and now I have a bit of that power!" Vesha says as her eyes glow evermore intensely.

"I earned what I have, and you know it. Had you been the better then you would be with him but that is not the case. You failed and I prevailed so spare me the everyone should be a winner story; victories are hard fought and earned. So bring it so that I can continue slapping you around!" Shabazz replies as Vesha rushes forth.

This time she tackles Shabazz taking her legs out, but Shabazz delivers elbows repeatedly across the back and spine of Vesha. She takes little notice of the blows and strikes Shabazz, even though the blow is blocked it still drops Shabazz to one knee. Shabazz performs an acrobatic flip kick catching Vesha in the chin. She staggers back and Hera injects her with a chemical that attacks her Hemoglobin. For the moment she becomes dizzy and light-headed, enraged she turns to deal with Hera. She snatches Hera by the shirt and throws her violently; Shabazz catches Hera and crashes through a building door. Preventing what would have surely been a fatal blow to the already injured Hera.

The other war continues, with Relick and Drazor and it is heated as cops join the fight but are overwhelmed with the attacking demons and dead as the people continue to stampede trying to avoid being eaten or drug to hell.

"This is getting bad, we need to end this but these bastards are pretty tough he has the chaos gem and that other cat is a force of nature. Still don't know what that shining thing in the sky is, but it's getting closer?" Relick says as he moves to attack Set and Combaticus.

"Ok just let me try this on old snake face, then you can have 'em, cool? Just let me get this thing ready" Drazor replies as he takes what appears to be an elastic compound and attaches C-4 to a slab of concrete.

"You got it, yo Combaticus can I have a word?" Relick asks.

When Combaticus turns to face Relick, Relick is already airborne with both hands clasped together. He brings them down hand in a hammer strike across the head of Combaticus. The force is so powerful that Combaticus is slammed through the surface and into the sewers. His dead followers then begin their attack on Relick this is stupid and fruitless as Relick makes this nine to five seem more like thirty minutes. The cops become possessed by the demonic entitles, and they begin attacking the humans, firing shot after shot killing many. Some cops resist the urge to kill another innocent and kill themselves. Relick then deals with the cops that want to kill proving that this is their true nature, and he is unkind because they are beyond help, mercy is not shown. Set however is sneaking up behind Relick intending to ambush him.

"Hey Relick duck!" Drazor yells as he fires his concrete C-4 infused missile at Set.

Set notices it a bit too late, as the projectile seems to take his head off. He catches the bomb in his serpentine mouth, it begins to beep then it explodes slamming him into his demon entourage. Drazor is pleased but is caught unaware Combaticus has broken through the sewer and back to the surface. He is caring a stone spiked club fashioned from stone and strikes Drazor in the arm damaged by Set. He is knocked to the ground and Combaticus begins to pummel him with the mighty weapon. He breaks Drazors arm and strikes him several times in the head. He stands and begins to stomp Drazors bloody body, for good measure he jabs the club into the body of Drazor like he was a post-hole digger. Relick is in shock and attacks Combaticus with unmatched ferocity. Combaticus swings his club and Relick catches it, and viciously punches Combaticus in the throat, and sends him flying back with a paralyzing upper cut, he follows with a left, right hook combo to the head and body. Combaticus can barely stand as each punch shatters windows. He falls to his knees and then onto his side, Relick is then hit with a blast he is all too familiar with the Crimson Chaos blast from Set. This stuns Relick, as Set cuts his uniform with his corrosive ax Death, Asp. Set places Relick in a head lock, like lighting Relick counters with an aerial backdrop that leaves Set folded over like a patio chair. Relick steps on Set's hand and prevents him from swinging the dreaded ax, then Relick grabs Set's slobbering mouth and rips It open. Set screams in pain and fires a Chaos blast point blank in the face of Relick; Relick is thrown back from the blast while holding his face in serious discomfort.

Set feeling that the downed Relick is a sign of victory fires a Chaos Blast a the downed Combaticus. Combaticus is bathed in the waves of energy and he can no longer move as Set stands above all the other fallen warriors. Set looks to the sky as some of the few remaining airplanes try to leave the area to catch his eye. Energy is charging the air and the strange glowing light begins to brighten and move closer to the battleground. The energy begins to disrupt all nearby electronics as if an EMP has been set off. The planes begin to lose power and fall to the ground, killing hundreds.

"NO!" Relick yells as he tries to stand.

He takes to the air as a 747 plane is falling to its doom weakened by the battle he catches the plane and strains to slow its descent. The glowing form begins to take on a humanoid shape, it then just hovers above and starts firing energy all the demons are neutralized. Set is concerned because he can sense the incredible power that this thing has.

"You have finally done it Set you will have to deal with the one force none can stand against no mercy will be given to you and that gem will not save you!" Combaticus says as he begins to smile.

"I fear none, I put you down and the guardian of this planet nothing is more powerful than I, Even your false God!" Set replies

Set fires every weapon in his arsenal striking the entity, it is unfazed faceless turns its head to Set and slices off his arm. Set bellows out, but the entity is not done administering pain he reaches into the open wound of Set and begins to dig around into the body of Set. He throws Set to the ground, with his remaining arm slices the ground opening the earth up and the entity falls into the opening. Set gloats as he begins to grow a new arm, the entity appears behind him and smashes the Gem of Chaos into hundreds of pieces and mangles the remaining hand of Set.

"Set do you realize what you are facing now? It is the end of all, he has wiped out all of your so-called Gods you are no different!"

Fear grips Set and Relick is also afraid he has just watched the entity decimate Set and smash the Gem of Chaos a feat that is not easily done. The plane has been slowed but the landing is still going to be a rough one, as he cuts a path through an abandoned part of town trying to land the plane. Passengers are thrown about the plane but luckily they all survive with minor injuries. Relick checks to make sure everyone is ok, then he gets a call from Warcast on his earpiece comlink.

"Relick you need to know what you are dealing with, this is the true destroyer of worlds he comes to purge galaxies when our creator has seen enough and there is no hope for redemption!" Warcast says

"Spit it out man, what is this thing I know it's biblical but what am I dealing with?" Relick asks

"This is the one fight you can not win, he is here to kill us all. He is the Arch Angel Michael, the right hand of GOD challenge him and you will die, my friend. I know that will not stop you because this is what you are born to do. I will make my peace with the creator; I do not dare challenge his word, his law the only law that matters. Man is the only one that changes; I will accept the punishment that we deserve. Please do not think me a coward?" Warcast says.

Relick pauses for a moment, the one force that he has prayed to his entire life he has to challenge for the fate of the universe, one of the few things that he fears. Never would he ever challenge an agent of the Lord. This is what he was born to do he will sacrifice any, and everything for his GOD, now he has come to his decision.

"I will fight, I am the only one who can, I know you can hear the explosions in the background. I'm two miles away, he is tearing Set apart, and basically torturing him for his defiance even shattering the Chaos Gem. Combaticaus has not moved he is Michael's agent obviously. My friend, I don't think that for one minute you are a coward you went into hell to liberate Cobalt's soul. Don't get anymore braver than that. I'm not going to survive this, do me one favor let my mother know who I was what I stood for, and let her know that I forgive her for all the pain she caused me. That I loved her and I always felt the pain, the deep pain that my father caused her. I'm sorry I look so much like him, and I apologize for him. To battle with you, my friend has been an honor, I go now to my death!"Relick replies as he is flooded with emotion, and that hard-to-swallow feeling in his throat. He does the only thing he can and that is to pray, pray for GOD to have mercy on his soul.

Warcast tries to answer, but Relick cuts the transmission as he streaks to the battlefield.

Chapter 6

Reckoning

Set is begging for his life and Michael continues to stalk him, Set tries to open a portal to escape. He thinks that he is successful as he enters, the tunnel of energy, but at the end of this tunnel, the faceless head of Michael the Arch Angel blocks his escape and on the other side where Set originally left. The Arch Angel has reached into the portal pulling Set out by the back of the neck. A sword is then drawn by the angel and he begins to carve Set up into pieces, he throws the dead corpse of Set along with the other body parts into the portal then it is sealed. All the people stand in horror some fall to their knees while others stand in pure horror for in life they never knew GOD, believed that he was myth and legend. One or two evaporate as according to scripture while those that remain are blinded and sucked into the vortex tossing them into the seven-headed dragon's waiting mouth. Then tremendous energy is fired at the sinners and non-believers, Relick in the nick of time blocks the blast but at a heavy causing his nervous system to all but shut down only the Gem of Destiny is restoring him. However, it is taking a long time in doing so.

"Run get out of here, move, damn it this is not a drill!" Relick yells

"You can't run from GOD, I'm too scared to run!" Bystander says.

Omnipotus moves closer as the ground quakes, Relick draws upon his courage and activates his force field, Omnipotus walks right through it. Relick stands to fight for the people when out of nowhere a blue streaking metallic hawk grabs Omnipotus dragging him from the battle for the time being and slamming him to the ground. It is Horus Relicks immortal guardian.

"Horus they said he killed all the Gods, what are you doing here not that I'm complaining?" Relick asks with a smile on his face.

"I had been told to stay out of this, but I'm your protector and friend we will die here today but not without a fight. I have already asked GOD for forgiveness. The Rapture has claimed but another Hera is removed and Shabazz is fighting Vesha to the death!" Horus replies he is grabbed by unseen energies and held in place, and he is being crushed it is Omnipotus.

"Let him go!" Relick screams as he lifts two dump trucks and claps Omnipotus between them attempting to crush him.

Again Ommipotus is not bothered but drops Horus anyway.

The fight between Shabazz and Vesha rages on, Shabazz is down because her focus is split because of what is happening to Relick and

Horus. She knows that if Horus is here then this is a very grim situation.

"Wanna help him so bad don't you, you can't even help your own shit here with me!" Vesha says as she attacks Shabazz again.

Shabazz throws electrified bolos at Vesha binding her hands and feet, and then a current is sent through her body. Vesha begins to flop on the ground from the voltage.

"It would seem that our battle needs a recess!" Shabazz responds

Omnipotus rises high over the city to end it he powers up; the sky begins to cover over with strangely shaped clouds as the planet starts to shake violently. Fire, brimstone, and lightning strike below bombarding pedestrians, buildings, cars, and trees none will be spared.

"YOU CAN NOT ALLOW HIM TO REACH CRITICAL MASS, I HAVE SEEN HIM DO THIS ALL OVER THE PLANET. ONCE HE DOES THAT CITY OR COUNTRY IS NO MORE!" Horus yells.

Relick powers up drawing on the Gem of Destiny's full power, he then rockets to Omnipotus full speed and delivers the most powerful punch he has ever thrown. The punch lands hard, stunning Omnipotus. It seems as though the tide has turned.

"Lord, did I do it?" Relick asks.

He is quickly answered Omnipotus shakes off the attack that would have shattered a planet, but now he powers up and massive wings from his back appear in all their glory. Suddenly he strikes Relick with a blow so powerful that it seems to cancel out sound, buildings and surfaces alike are peeled back slowly. The effect resembles a low-yield nuke, Relick is sent falling to the earth like a flaming meteorite, and the impact is gargantuan as Relick is lying motionless in a hole that would make the Grand Canyon jealous. Horus is stunned and unable to move, the raw power of Omnipotus has taken much from him. Shabazz watches in terror!

"RELICK!" Shabazz screams as she tries to run to his broken body, but she is grabbed by Vesha she too is overcome with grief at the sight of Relick being downed and presumably dead.

"IF I WERE HIS PROTECTOR THIS WOULD NEVER HAVE HAPPENED, I AM GOING TO KILL YOU FOR THIS!" Vesha says as she places Shabazz in what she believes is an unbreakable chokehold.

"This is your end Vesha now know my rage as that monster will!" Shabazz replies

Shabazz drops to the ground losing the hold, she springs up head butting Vesha under the chin. With the Fist of Destiny hand still glowing strikes Vesha in Forty-two different pressure points on her body, causing complete organ failure. Her muscles are rendered ridge. With one punch Shabazz reaches into the chest of Vesha and tears her heart out, the eyes of Vesha roll to the back of her head. She manages to make one last statement.

"A one-handed ass whipping impressive!" Vesha says as she falls face first to the blacktop as her final breath leaves her body.

Shabazz looks at Relick and activates both Fists of Destiny, people run past her and she fights her way to Relick who has blood coming from his mouth, nose, ears, and eyes she can barely look at him as she holds him in her arms. She is then challenged by a few demons that intend to kill her; this will be a move that they will come to regret. As she slowly drags Relick to a quick safe point, Shabazz throws down a smoke bomb that has silver and salt combined at the feet of the demons, they stagger and cough violently as they inhale the blinding mist. Shabazz strikes she slaps explosives with spiked attachments to the backs of some and simply punches through the bodies of others. She activates the charges, and the demons explode Shabazz never even looks back. Others simply fall having their heads removed and chests opened up by her mighty blows. She turns her attention back to the downed Relick again placing him on her upper thigh as she sits down, running her hand across his face. She believes the worst has happened.

"Is he…?" Horus asks as he is still unable to move.

"He is not breathing!" Shabazz replies as Omnipotus levitates toward them.

Shabazz kisses Relick on the forehead and gently lays him down, she cries and then screams to the heavens.

Omnipotus attempts to grab Relick, but only Shabazz is not having any of it.

"YOU WILL NOT TOUCH HIM, I WILL KILL YOU DEAD FOR WHAT YOU HAVE DONE TO HIM. WAR WITH ME!" Shabazz says as she punches Omnipotus he is knocked back and appears to be dazed.

Shabazz does not let up she continues with every fighting style known to man, and she appears to be winning. The sheer force of pure love has amplified her power level, Omnipotus is reeling from the most powerful force in the universe, love is challenging one of the most powerful forces ever conceived. Omnipotus is down on one knee trying to get his bearings, Shabazz moves in for the kill. She is struck by energy from the hands of Omnipotus. Shards of glass and debris strike her damaged uniform cutting it she begins to punch at the barrage. She leaps and jaw crunches Omnipotus he spins to the left, and with unseen energy, he applies force to move Shabazz backward. Shabazz against all odds pushes forward; the loss of Relick pushes her beyond human levels she continues to move until she can no longer progress. Omnipotus then reaches for her, Horus is finally able to move again and attacks Omnipotus stunned at the determination of the last two remaining beings he fires lightning electrocuting both of them. Time stops as the two are frozen caught in the electro static deluge, Relick has time paused and pulled the two from harm's way, but this may have cost him. Although time has stopped for all things around them, Omnipotus is unaffected by it he is not at all impressed. He strikes the already broken Relick; dropping him, Relick is rendered useless in the fight.

"For once I've saved you guys!" Relick says in a weakened voice. As Omnipotus grabs him he looks back at the two, as he is flung across the skyline.

"NOOOOOOOOOOOO!" Shabazz screams as she watches Relick sail out of sight.

Shabazz is refueled with new rage, which has again increased her power, strength, and resolves. She yells and strikes Omnipotus with a roundhouse kick, a back fist, and a final flying dagger kick. Horus adds by hitting him with an enormous energy blast and then tackles him to the ground. The two warriors attack simultaneously and begin to ground and pound Omnipotus.

"For what you just did to him, I WILL HAVE YOUR HEART ON MY FIST'S MONSTER, YOU WILL PAY!" Shabazz says as she strikes Omnipotus with everything she has.

"SHE SPEAKS THE TRUTH, THOUGH WE MAY DIE HERE TODAY YOU WILL SURELY BE JOINING US!" Horus adds as the two pour it on for the apparent death of their friend.

Suddenly Omnipotus begins to glow and grow to a staggering twenty feet, he expels Shabazz and Horus from his outer shell. The two roll back, and take a readied stance, Omnipotus hovers upward and the sky once again changes. Energy is released striking Horus and Shabazz dodges the projected energies. Horus is down as he has his armor ripped from his body, he is being burned to a divine crisp. Then the focus is turned to Shabazz.

"I DO NOT FEAR YOU OR DEATH THIS FIGHT IS FOR RELICK DAMN YOU!" Shabazz screams as she charges forward braving the death that will surely take her. It matters not for her best friend is gone she has nothing to live for.

Suddenly there is an incredibly bright light that stops her in mid-motion, as the energy is directed back at Omnipotus giving him pause for the moment. The wind picks up as tornados, fire, rain, and ice blades ravage the surface. Explosions from generators, power lines, and cars erupt all around Shabazz. She blocks incredible amounts of the bombardment with her fists still energized, but she is removed from surface contact by the powerful winds. Now airborne Shabazz is forced left to right, up and down, by the incredible display of power from Omnipotus. Until out of the blinding light that redirected

Omnipotus's energy, an arm that appears to be vapor catches her. She is now stabilized; she is relieved for the form is known to her.

They are the mighty vapors, Urodon the Ultimate, Heczar the Hammer, Elcum the Onynx. Normally they would stay their hands in the affairs of humanity, but Urodon will not let Shabazz fall alone. The three stand as one when such a foe presents itself but never has a foe of this magnitude been seen in such modern times and they know exactly what is going at hand here.

"I will not allow you to do battle alone, we are here though this foe is all powerful you again have shown a level that none in your kind has ever displayed before! Urodon says as he stands ready for battle.

"This being was seen at the birth of Christ, the star that guided the three wise men Christ birth!" Heczar replies as he appears from smoke form.

"This being you face now was sent by GOD, to protect the Messiah from any and all demonic harm. When he has made his appearance in the past it is always a most serious issue with our Lord GOD!" E-clum adds

"We are those three wise men that are spoken about in the Bible that made the venture to bear witness and protect the baby Jesus as well. This is not a battle we can win!" Urodon says

"Never would we dare to challenge our Lord and Master, but we have stayed in the shadows too long!" Heczar replies.

"Perhaps we can show that we are worthy of a chance for redemption, if not we have made our peace with GOD and will join the fate of the rest of the universe!" E-clum adds.

The maelstrom that is raging around them only moves their garbs; the wind is causing their strange materials to flow majestically in the wind. The trio attacks and it is immense, Heczar seems to have blinded Omnipotus with an energy hammer to the face, Urodon spins him in a vortex of divine energy, and E-clum throws him to the surface of the earth violently. The three circles above him in a triangle, rotating in an erratic pattern, but this does not last, not one more moment of calm will be allowed. Omnipotus streaks through the trio like a phoenix reborn, striking each with debilitating energy especially attuned to disrupting each of them. They fall to the streets, shaken but able to continue the battle. The strangeness in the sky and environment does not subside but doubles, the Vapors make one last ultimate play to stay Omnipotus.

"He will not stop, until this planet is destroyed, I will restore Horus!" E-clum says as he energies the fallen god.

"You must find the Akashic Record, it may yet still hold some clue to help you against this foe we have lost this battle, but we will see it through!" Heczar says as they all begin to glow and power up.

"If Relick is dead you will still need to find the Gem of Destiny, to help you because there is one other that can use it, I will restore the Gem of Chaos

so that you will have the two. Once you can find the Akashic Record, you will need both. Horus remove Shabazz from the battlegrounds you can do no more here!" Urodon says as Shabazz hugs him

Urodon touches the forehead of Shabazz giving her the location of the Akashic Record. Horus stands behind Shabazz and touches her shoulder engulfing her in his transportation energies. But not before the two witnesses the merging of the three vapors into one being of pure might and considerable size. With the arms of E-clum, the body of Heczar, and the head of Urodon, they slightly glance at Shabazz and Horus as they take flight. There is one last subconscious message given to Shabazz and Horus. GO! The combined might of the Vapors streak to Omnioptus as he in turn attacks back they meet in the middle and there is a blinding bright light. It is the last thing that Shabazz and Horus see as they teleport away, for unbeknownst to them the states of Louisiana, Texas some parts, but all of San Antonio, Mississippi are no more because of the explosion. The world is coming to an end!

Chapter 7

Unchecked Pathogens equal Atrophy

Indianapolis In. In the famous Indy 500, we find Tacea scoping out the area for the two remaining Horsemen of the apocalypse, Pathogen, and Atrophy. The crowd would be perfect for an attack, a chance to spread death and break open the seals. The last members of the Celestial Seven don't even know the fate of the others, but will soon find out.

"Well, I really don't get this driving in a circle I mean really what could possibly drag this many people to watch this? Please don't tell me this is a sport cause I'm just gonna laugh till I vomit, how are you doing over there? "Tacea says to Housequake over the comlink.

"Same shit different toilet, and I won't because we don't need you doing all that now do we, but I totally agree not a sport more like a Redneck get-together is how I see it. Housequake responds.

"I haven't seen any signs and this tracker hasn't blinked or bleaked once. How is Vegas hope you having more fun than I am, this shit blows hard. Have you heard from Relick or Shabazz? Tacea asks.

"No not yet, wait, wait a minute, speak of the Devil no pun intended. It's Warcast let me call you back Quake out. Housequake replies as he answers the incoming call.

"I have some rather bad news, to convey to you, I believe Relick is dead! Warcast says.

"How that Horseman kill 'em? Housequake asks.

"No, you should have seen him, neither Set nor Combaticus could do much with Relick. In combat he was magnificent, he has…had really evolved in his usage and fighting skills, you would have been quite proud!" Warcast replies.

"Spill it DAMN IT, let me know who I have to kill, somebody's gonna pay for this. Where is Shabazz, is she good?" Housequake asks.

"This thing I don't believe can be stopped or killed, this is a being of divinity. So powerful was this thing that, he all but dropped Relick with one blow. The orb that I used to view the battle was almost destroyed by the spillage of power from the blow. So powerful is this being, the god Horus had to intervene, but equally, put down was he. Warcast says.

"So what the hell is this thing that could do that to those two, where is Shabazz man how is she taking this?" Housequake asks anxiously awaiting a response.

"This thing is the Bringer of Death, the Arch Angel Michael, GOD's right hand. He tortured Set even with the full power exerted by the Gem of Chaos, he made Set crawl like a dog. Shabazz, however, did not take the battle well, but for some bizarre reason, she was able to affect the being known as Omnipotous Aka Michael. She went into a rage, and battled him to a standstill; he had to power up incredibly just to slow her assault. Never have I witnessed a more pure combatant, she was otherworldly in her attack on him. Last I saw was her being knocked back, in a blinding flash my orb could not take the power surge it was outright destroyed!" Warcast says.

"I…take it you have a plan we still need to track down these other fuckers right?" How can I break this to Tacea, you know how she is about this kinda of thing. I'm gonna break those punks, mark that! Why didn't you help, don't you have like some really powerful, Merlin types in your corner?" Housequake asks.

"We had an understanding, my mission was to go to hell and retrieve Cobalt's soul. We did that, but the most vexing part is that he and Outrage once the mission was near over, vanished into thin air. When we arrived, hell had no master just unchecked evil. Lucifer was his first target it was a quick battle that's why hell has no leader. It is part of the Rapture biblical level events; there is no one that can deal with Omnipotous. This is evident in the manner in which he dispatched our planet's ultimate protector. For the time the whereabouts of Shabazz are unknown. Would not be wise to tell Tacea for the moment keep her in the dark about this, my friend!" Warcast says as they both become silent for the moment.

"Alright I guess you are right, you say I our boy went out like a champ?" Housequake asks trying to remain hopeful.

"Like a titan of old, my good man completely fearless, he will sorely be missed for what time we have left!" Warcast responds proudly

"Good to know true warrior, ultimate General, keep me updated Quake out!" Housequake says as he ends the communication.

"I don't care who that thing is, Lord please forgive me I mean no disrespect but Michael or Omnipotus is gonna pay for this!" Housequake says while speaking in a low voice to GOD.

His com-link begins to vibrate, it's Tacea she wants an update as to what is happening and the next move for them.

"Ok so what's the gossip spill it, how is everybody doing with their missions? Tacea asks.

"They are fine, good even they have accomplished their parts in this so now it's our turn to do 'em one better. These slot machines are acting funny, and my tracker is giving off some strange readings. Give me five minutes I'll get back to you, let me check something real quick! Housequake replies.

"Ok bro you got five minutes you're making me nervous, I want some action. We got to get some leads on this thing!" Tacea says

As the communication is stopped, the air is distorted so Quake does the norm, he scouts around the area to see if he can find the issue. People are on the slot machines trying for the chance to break the bank. But one individual looks a bit out of place in the charged environment. The bone structure and facial features are disturbing; still, it sits playing the slot machine along with the other guest. They seem to be totally oblivious to the odd man.

"So are you gonna just stare at me the whole time or ask those deeply burning questions about the hereafter?" The entity asks.

Startled that it noticed him Housequake sits down cautiously in the empty slot machine seat next to it.

"Which one are ya, the stinky one or the sick one?" Housequake replies.

"Ouch… you humans are rude, ok I'll play. I'm the hungry one, I have pimped many names in my time Famine, and most recently Atrophy. It suits the times at hand don't you agree, the decline of society, etc., etc.?" Atrophy says as he tosses a few coins for Housequake to play with.

"Now which one of you is responsible for killing my friend Relick, you know the drill someone's gonna pay!" Housequake asks as he pulls on the handle of the slot machine.

"You a gambling man huh? You are next to one of the prophets of the apocalypse, and yet you are not nervous or affected by me…Hmm curious what makes you so bold?"

Atrophy says as he sniffs in the direction of Housequake.

"Ah got it you have divine incantations, and charms powerful magic. I wonder if you can still take a direct touch, oh well later after we've had our lil chitchat. Isn't this just peachy two regular Joe's playing the slot machines, discussing the end of all things? Exciting don't you think?" Atrophy taunts.

"Which one chump, I ain't got all day? You think that we're just gonna lay down without a fight…? Then you don't know us very well then, and I know damn well my friend went out the same way!?" Housequake says.

"Oh dear, he was the most powerful person in your world, and maybe, just maybe a few more if he learned how to harvest the gem of destiny. It's really powerful…well was powerful. You things, humans pardon me, crawl around acting like the best thing since cheesecake. How long did you think you could continue acting this way, it was bound to end and be messy. Whatever made you great, you gave up on it, sacrificed all of it for what? Guess you forgot about

GOD huh still don't know what he saw in you. You worship a flag built on hate in the south of this country but say that it's part of your heritage. William T. Thompson in 1863 damn sure didn't make it for that purpose. He claims GOD told the white man to enslave the black man when I clearly remember him saying let my people go. I should know I was one of the plagues during the Exodus!" Atrophy replies.

"So you were there at the time of Moses?" Housequake asks.

"My dear lil boy I have been around since the first thing in existence had an expiration date! Now what killed your friend is more powerful than anything you can imagine, we are but the first wave. Look around at the people here, they look really hungry!" Atrophy says as he pulls on the lever of his slot machine, a woman is starting to eat her own arm at the blackjack table but she's not noticed yet.

"So you are doing this just by being in the building?" Housequake asks.

"Ding, ding give that boy a prize, everyone here is going to die. Either from accelerated cellular degeneration or tearing each other apart in a starvation fit of rage. It will be beautiful, just wait you've never seen anything like this!" Atrophy responds.

Housequake is now starting to understand just what they are up against; all of the horsemen are equally as powerful. He still has questions that need answers.

"Why not just stop this crap, isn't there another way we can change. All the prayers not all of us have thrown away our faith, Relick died for his faith and all of us doesn't that count for something?" Housequake asks while pulling on his machine's lever.

"Stop it, stop it too many chances have been given, hell it was the prayers of the few that kept this from going to shit a long time ago. Most of them have ascended to heaven, or whatever place of peace their culture might have called it. Let me show you, you have a government that for over 400 years would allow a group of people to be slaughtered because of skin color. Now they are not perfect none of you are but you use fear of white sheets with holes in them torch burning and crosses. Never understood that concept of the sheets, a group of chaw chewing white men on horses running burning things! Even have the balls to burn down churches, now those same hate mongers hide behind government jobs, and the military, and wait for its drums to roll, please…COPS more directly the "White male cops", not all but, many too many. Truly a land where the sons of Cane are in droves here his blood runs deep. Only fitting that then end starts here, many chances to stop the behavior but you didn't." Atrophy says

"Come on now they don't speak for us all some of us fight against that shit!" Housequake responds.

"Really even when you have video footage of the white people, that's what you call yourselves. Still trying to make excuses for the demonic behavior, and few if any stand up and say enough already. You know that was the final seal that unleashed us uh huh… Did you know that? What do you think would happen if blacks attacked you, white people? Hanged you, castrated you, oppressed you, killed you in cold blood we've seen the footage I have it all on VHS, or is it BETA? You even have postcards that show your people gathered around the burning bodies, hanging bodies of blacks while eating, and having what you call pick-nicks. But then my tape gets blurry and fuzzy really need to transfer them over to Blu-ray, you know for prosperity!" Then deny you justice how would you react to that huh?" Well, have you seen the movie "White Mans Burden" starring John Travolta? That's totally what you would do. I got that on VHS wanna borrow it?" Atrophy says

"I don't know what to say, guess we got it coming I can accept that!" Housequake responds.

"My dear bubble head, like you have a choice either way, still think you are in charge huh? Well, I've had my fun this machine is not gonna give up any profit. So let's do our part of ending your kind, oh look it's already starting. Can you believe it, that woman is using hot sauce on that guy's back? I believe her friend is eating his ass area. Hungry lil devils aren't they?" Atrophy taunts.

Housequake is in shock as he looks on at the decline of humanity he fires tear gas trying to break the ravagers up but this is biblical it's beyond him. So he tries another measure.

"STOP THIS SHIT I KNOW YOU CAN!" Housequake yells.

"Or what I can see behind those tiny lil eyes there is an ultimatum if I don't. Still think you are in control you germs are so funny!" Atrophy says while laughing hysterically.

Angry and desperate, Quake does what Quake does. His arm transforms into a plasma cannon and he blows Atrophy through the side of the Casino.

"Ain't no fun when the rabbit got the gun is it PUNK!" Housequake replies, his cannon still smoking!

"Tacea we have a problem I've found the bum Atrophy the bible calls em Famine of the Horsemen. He's infected the whole casino, the people are tearing each other apart!" Housequake says to Tacea via their communications link.

"Well damn how bad is it, 'cause it's getting pretty weird here too? Bet it's the last one nothing else left people are getting really sick, 250,000 sick" Tacea responds.

"He seems to be coming back for more, I might need your help locking into my GPS, Quake out!"

"Owwwie, you play hard, let me sic the dogs on you gotta join my brother in Indiana. My work here is done!" Atrophy says as his starvation-crazed savage begin to attack Housequake, Atrophy vanishes.

Quake readies himself but notices that a path has been cut bodies are flying all over the casino.

"Was that fast enough, had to pitch a few coins in the toll booths across America?" Tacea replies.

"On the money as usual young lady, we gotta get to Indy they gonna team up and end us all! Housquake says.

"Hold on let's get gone, time to bitch slap some freaks!" Tacea replies as she streaks away with Housequake.

The brain-dead people have all but destroyed the building and each other. Man's decline is almost complete the spared fortuned have already been pulled from this area. Pity them not; pity those that are left to bear witness to the end of all. The horror has just started.

Tacea cannot exert full speed because Housequake's body could not withstand the G-force nor the friction. Her speed in getting them back to Indiana is impressive nonetheless. As they arrive the area is turning into the same blood bath that, was evident in Las Vegas. Now they must locate the two responsible, but that won't take long not in the least bit.

"What are we looking for, anything special just let me know what I need to break or hit?" Tacea asks.

"Well, I know what Atrophy looks like, and I'm pretty sure with a name like Pathogen not gonna be hard to figure 'em out. I imagine him or it looking like this fat nasty reject of a Marine I knew named Marc Barkly, he was such a poor soldier. The fat slob had the nerve to tell me that he wished that he could cut his Marine tattoo off. He is a disgusting disgrace to the men he served with, don't get me wrong the government is full of shit, but you went in with a so-called band of soldiers that thought he had their backs if they only knew. Heard he had a security position at Hamsung technologies, they tell me that his fat ass weighs about 380 lbs. Sweats just standing outside even in the shade, he pushes his weight around violating every protocol just to justify his job position. Placing the people that work with 'em in very bad situations, how slime like 'em gets away with it is beyond me, the fat fuck!" Housequake says as they look at the slowly transforming crowd of 250,000.

"I neva could stand people like that, and they always seem to make it off the backs of the lil people. Here and now that should change because all people like that can see the dark hole that they have dug for themselves, and ain't no changing that!" Tacea replies.

"He expects everybody to do work he won't do, what kinda leader is that? Neva expect a person to do what you know damn well know you won't do yourself!" Housequake says their opponents have made their way to the concession area.

As they intend to infect the food and people by any means necessary. People start to drop and change into human cannibals courtesy of Atrophy. Pathogen has an even nasty effect on the crowd, sores, and boils, burn and burst onto others quickly spreading his disease. Once infected they become mindless roaming creatures that are removed totally from their human qualities, fingernails crack and bleed or pop off from the fingers, eyes, and ears leak blood and other sickening fluids. They vomit spewing massive piles of pus many fall dead from the touch of Pathogen. He reveals himself and he is large and as grotesque as one might imagine from the creature responsible for all of mankind's viruses, germs, and epidemics.

"Well just because you requested it, here I am and I will take on the form you just spoke about to get under your skin. It's not like I'm not already there anyway!" Pathogen says coughing and saliva flowing from his mouth.

"Man, just nine kinds of nasty aren't ya…well we like to kick the shit out of nasty. You just like a big nasty zit with a wig on it, give me a second I'll be over there in a minute to pull it right off your fat head!" Tacea replies, as she is about to run to do business she is stopped and warned by Housequake.

"Hold on, these bumps are straight from the bible, I shot that other cat fat in the face point blank. Blew 'em clean through the side of the building but…" Housequake says almost until he is interrupted.

"But here I stand dear boy, love you manners, and who might this lovely young thing be? You should so introduce us, I am Atrophy and you are?" Atrophy asks.

"Well I'm the thing that likes to break her foot off in weirdos, and you so fit the bill of weirdo!" Tacea replies.

"Bravo you humans are so funny even at the end of all things, we are here so you know he is here. I know that your other team members, know that in full now since he killed them and tore them apart!" Atrophy says to the bewildered look on the face of Tacea.

"What the hell is he talking about Quake?" Tacea asks as she turns to him expecting an answer.

"What big boy didn't tell you? Just so you know they put up an outstanding fight the best I've seen in this part of the universe. But when he shows up there: can be only one outcome, don't worry they died honorably all but Set!" Atrophy says.

"He Warcast told me not to tell you to stay on point we have a mission to complete. He knows how emotional you can get, and we need to stop something. The horsemen have been weakened by the others each time they have been defeated, but there is this one thing that stopped Relick cold. From what Warcast said it is the Right hand of God Michael the angel. Nothing was stopping our boy until Michael arrived!" Housequake says.

"Oh man, what about Shabazz, is she ok?" Tacea asks.

"Not sure but it even put down Horus, we have a mission and we have got to get it done. See how emotional you're getting this is why he said to hold off telling you. But rest on it, these two fuckers are gonna pay for what they did to our friends!" Housequake says.

"You so got that right, this ain't gonna ride without you BITCHES GETTING THE SHIT KICKED OUTTA YOU!" Tacea replies as she powers up.

"Now this is what I love about you microbes, your last hours you still just won't lay it down. Oh this horde behind us do take it easy on them they are dead and damned, even the demons are trying to make a last sacking of the souls here! Pathetic creatures they are actually we hate them more than we hate you, arrogant humans!" Atrophy says as demons mix in with the infected virus spewing damned.

"I've been waiting for you, this could be stopped but if this is our last fight you best believe that it will be one that even you will be talking about forever!" Housequake says as he morphs his arms to fire blessed projectile armaments.

"I GONNA BREAK YOU DOGS!" Tacea yells as she places blessed iron knuckles on her hands.

She explodes into the crowd, smashing everything in sight like a hyperactive pinball machine. From the top of a nearby building, it looks like the fourth of July, as the bodies in the infected area spark and burst into flames of multiple color schemes. Housequake fires at a wave of demons that climb over one another trying to collect his soul. They are met with a holy bombardment that has them all exploding all over the surface area. He morphs his arms from, plasma weapons to, M-60s, Iron Javelins, to the famous Jackhammers. His transformations are smooth and fluid as he pummels all incoming attackers.

"You over there laughing Atrophy? Well, let me give you something to cry about. TACEA NOW! Housequake yells.

Tacea in a blink is standing next to the gruesome twosome, and she punches them both with a blow not seen in a while her Taceon punch. The blow is powerful, and enhanced by the blessed weapons on her hands they are sent flying towards the awaiting Housequake. He smashes Atrophy between his Jackhammered fists, and in what seems like slow motion crushes Pathogen into the pavement.

"Not so ha, ha now is it punk you got more coming now get your asses up, THE PAIN IS JUST BEGINNING! Tacea yells, as the horde continues she does what she does.

She grabs a rope, cords, and anything she can to bind or tie the incoming hordes. For her time has slowed down as she streaks in and out killing all that is in her line of sight she seems to be at two places at once. Her incredible speed is overwhelming the monsters as they drop and their numbers begin to dwindle. Atrophy and Pathogen re-enter the battle and make a bid to increase the beasts.

"That was damned impressive human, but either of you that we touch directly will be the end for you. So come on fast track let's see what you got?" Pathogen says.

"You got it, nasty fat boy!" Tacea replies she attacks so fast and takes the legs out from under the two.

They fall and she runs from one to the other giving them both an iron-knuckled styled muggy. The speed at which she has done this makes a groove in the head of Pathogen, and he screams as his gray matter is falling out from the opening she has made. Atrophy has a different reaction; his head catches on fire he tries in vain to put it out. Housequake seizes the moment and unloads with every weapon at his disposal as Tacea streaks out of the way; the hordes are cut down, and as there is a violent explosion, nothing moves except for the twitching body parts.

"Now this is where you assholes lay down, and cry uncle but assuming you are what Quake says you are it won't be that easy?" Tacea says.

"Oh I'm just hoping that they want another round, please say so!" Housequake says.

The two forces of nature stand and send the assault on the remaining demons to aid them, against these two imposing forces. They stand and move forward along with the stampeding hell spawns, and human infected. It seems as though the joking attitude of the horsemen are, gone and an approach of destruction has replaced all else.

"Oh yeah they want to get this done then don't they well let's not keep 'em waiting huh Quake?" Tacea says as she looks at Housequake.

"Yeah, but I wouldn't take my eyes off of them or turn my back for a minute to 'em!" Housequake replies, but before he can finish his sentence the fat one Pathogen now sporting glasses makes his move.

He begins to cough up a thick mucus-like substance and spits it onto the surface in front of him. With a hand smears it in a circle that forms a line that bolts towards the unsuspecting Tacea. She can't react as the surface around her become sick and brittle she has no way to get any momentum built to move.

"Damn it, girl I told you not to take your eyes off 'em, I got the demons!" Housequake says.

"Oh shit I know, I know but just give me a minute I'll figure it out!" Tacea replies as she looks around trying to crawl to the edge of the infected area.

"Come on you damned bastard I've got something for your asses!" Housequake says.

He changes his arm into a cannon and loads it with a special Chinese missile that wards off evil spirits. He fires above their heads, and they look up as the noise and fallout cause them tremendous pain. They all stop in their place and begin to fall to the ground writhing in their agony. This makes them easy targets for Housequake as he begins, to snipe the entire lot with blessed iron projectiles. They explode in multiple colors as the shots rip the bodies of the damned into shredded meat. Pathogen then lumbers towards a ten-story hotel and infects it with the same putrid liquid spewed from his mouth. He spreads it on the foundation of the building the bottom of the building turns black and brown. Some people that occupy the building try to leave and are quickly infected down to the bone and fall to the ground reduced to fluids and dust. The building becomes unstable and gives way falling towards Tacea who cannot move to evade because of the infected surface.

"TACEA GET YOUR ASS OUTTA THERE, THE BUILDING IS COMING DOWN ON YOU MOVE!" Housequake says as he fires rockets trying to break the building up before it strikes her.

Housequake is down to his last rocket, but he is too late the building collapses upon her.

"TACEAAAAAA!" Housequake screams as she is buried outright beneath tons of rubble.

"This is the second friend of mind that you've killed now before this is over you will either add me to this list or I'm gonna add you to the list of shit that I've killed over the years. SO THIS IS HOW IT'S GOING DOWN!" Housequake yells and morphs his arms into rotating uranium-tipped rocket launchers, and a plasma pulse laser rifle on the other arm, the remaining people scatter as million-dollar racecars are crashed and smoldering thousands are dead.

He is all that stands between the beings that are the signal to our end, he glances over to Tacea's last stand and readies his position as Atrophy and Pathogen to turn more of the scrambling crowd into slaughtering savages.

"My dear boy, such boisterous rhetoric, you still have no idea whom or what you are dealing with, this is the end of you everywhere. There is no escaping this, no reasoning, no tough talk; you germs brought this on yourselves!" Atrophy says with hands clasped behind his back.

"This is your fault how many have you killed in the name of duty and country? You have earned this!" Pathogen adds with his mouth dripping the sickness that plagues mankind.

"YOU SHUT YOUR FUCKING MOUTH BARKLY, YEAH I CALLED YOU BARKLY YOU FAT PIECE OF SHIT, YOU MAY NOT HIM BUT YOU STILL COME FROM THE SAME STINK THAT CRAPPED HIM OUT. I'M GONNA GET YOU, FAT BOY, FOR EVERYBODY THAT YOU SOLD OUT, LIED TO, FIRED, OR WHATEVER, COME TO THINK OF IT YOU ARE HIM, YEAH I SEE NOW YOU MAKE EVEN THE SOUL SICK!" Housequake replies.

"Guilty as charged, yeah it was me hiding out in a human form. Just to see what makes you new modern humans tick! To tell you the truth; all of my kind have been here in human form just for this reason. So what do you know been watching you for a while punk boy!" Pathogen says while virus infected slob drips from his mouth.

Housequake tries to target Atrophy and Pathogen, but the charging crowd is making it very difficult to target the monsters. People are falling around the area dying and just getting trampled. He knows that he can't save them all and with Tacea out of the picture it seems hopeless but he will not stop the fight!

"Move people get outta the damn way!" Housesquake yells as his targeting visor comes down trying to lock in on the horsemen.

His system quickly scans anything approaching him when a young lady he notices is pinned to the ground from the building that crushed Tacea. He reacts quickly to her and helps her in the dilemma that befell her.

"I got ya sweetie what's your name?" Housequake asks as he begins to lift the materials off her.

"D… Dee Wilson. I… can't move please don't let me die like this. OMG they are coming please get me outta here!" Dee begs.

"I got you just focus on me, now on the count of three pull your legs out ok and run down that way, and don't stop!" Housequake says.

"Ok please get me outta here fast!" Dee yells.

"One…Two…Three, move!" Housequake replies as he frees her.

"Thank you so much, be careful!" Dee says as she runs to the area Housequake pointed out!

She is clear; Housequake can now continue targeting the two forces of a natural order. His visor re-targets them scanning from weak points, but he has almost forgotten that he has blessed weaponry that makes every attack a weak point. So he just unloads, the plasma rifle rips into Atrophy, as he lumbers forth, but the uranium-tipped rounds he is all too happy to hit Pathogen with. Each explosion tears off chunks of flesh, Pathogen is screaming as the impact of each blessed round sends his mind into shock. But a few stragglers are still in the line of fire so he has to postpone the assault temporarily again.

"DAMN IT PEOPLE MOVE, YOU ARE GIVING THEM TARGETS TO USE AGAINST US GET OFF THE STREETS!" Housequake yells as the people take cover.

"I bet they wish that they had done better in life, if they had they would have ascended already don't you think good boy? As is once we touch them they are instruments to be used for our destruction, pity we are running out of the stupid's to use. Oh well, still have enough to deal with you. This is the part that we relish, killing your kind, the tough ones!" Atrophy says as he slams Housequake with energy and the Zom's try to pile on top of him.

Housquake fights them off, but no sooner than that is done Pathogen infects the leg of Quake.

"Blessed or not long exposure from a direct touch is going to affect you one way or another. Please believe me!" Pathogen adds as Housequakes leg becomes brittle with decay.

Quake fires plasma bolts point blank to the face of Pathogen sending him reeling backward and holding his face. He begins transforming his right arm into a jackhammer crashing into the back of Pathogen's head, smoothly planting his head into the surface of the street. But the damage is done; his neurological system is starting to shut down. He begins to cough violently, and as his eyes begin to water impairing his vision he stumbles back slowly regaining his bearings. His targeting systems in his visor go blank, he is essentially fighting blind.

"Very impressive you put down Pathogen, weakened and all that sort of thing!" Atrophy says laughing!

Housequake blasts him with the last uranium round he has left, leaving Atrophy in a cloud of smoke. The laughter has ceased for the moment.

"Little boy why don't you go to your room and fuck yourself, this is the big boy league and you just don't have permission to be in here!" Housequake replies as he staggers and falls to his knees.

"Seems as though you've just hit a rough patch, let me add to it brah this will only take a minute!" Pathogen says as he throws mucous from his mouth, hitting Quake in the chest.

This is no ordinary virus, this is a virus that eats the surface of any that it makes contact with. Quake is trying to remove the substance but it is too strong and now he is too weak. He falls to his back, as Atrophy makes his move. The virus has made Quake's armor open for attack, and he shoves his hand into the chest of Quake grabbing his heart. He accelerates the aging process to his heart, and Quake screams in pain.

"SHHHHH it won't be long dear boy, in a moment it will all be over, you put up one helluva fight you've represented the human race well. BUT NOW I REQUEST THAT YOU DIE!" Atrophy says while squeezing harder.

"That's ok it ain't…Quite over yet…you've just awakened something…Round two chumps!" Housequake says before he blacks out.

There is a loud hum and a vibration that shakes the surface, it has been unleashed the rubble that buried Tacea explodes violently! Tacea stands with a ferocious look the Sky Hammer has emerged.

"So you drop all this shit on me, try to kill me as you have done my friends, boys let me show you how I drop shit on people! Tacea says.

She begins to move one phase out of normal time, moving even faster than the two forces of nature can follow. For Atrophy, he knows what is to come, and with the enhanced blessing that she has this is a battle they cannot win. Tacea strikes.

"Oh, dear!" Atrophy says as she is in his personal space before he can process a thought.

"Since when do forces of nature mug people, that is what you are doing to my friend right?" Tacea replies.

She unleashes her ampt up Taceon punch to the body of Pathogen; a portion of his body disintegrates. He yells in pain as fluids from his body ooze from the opening Tacea has caused. With his remaining arm, he tries to heal himself but the punch has a residual deterioration effect that prevents this from happening.

"Atrophy what is this human, I can't heal what she hurt she was not this powerful before. I feel sick, I can't continue!" Pathogen says.

"Hold still boo, there's more for you, I gotta work on your friend now, you know slap the chuck wagon outta him!" Tacea responds.

She moves seemingly without the locomotion of her feet or any noticeable movement. She only seems to be in one place and then with a thought in another.

"Impossible for a mere germ to attain this kind of power so quickly, or even hide it as you have done from us dear girl!" Atrophy says.

In a blink, she is in the face of Atrophy and the damage to him is already done.

"Ok so for your sorry ass I've hit you with Four thousand nine hundred and fifty-eight punches. Your body is breaking down on a molecular level, you will be crapping your T.V. Dinner in about thirty-eight seconds. Shhh, don't say a word, you ain't gotta thank me I owed you for everybody that you dusted off today!" Tacea says as she stands back waiting for the breakdown of the force of nature to end.

"That's fine because once you stop us, he will come and finish what we have started, look up the sky is already preparing for his arrival. He killed your other friends, and he will show you no mercy, if I were you I would get your broken down chap over there and leave. Atrophy says as the sky turns every color imaginable.

The people and cars jam the area trying to escape the incoming terror, thunder, and lightning filling the sky. Suddenly there is an opening in the clouds a vortex has opened if you will. In a flash a powerful energy orb streaks to the battle area and strikes the area people are incinerated, cars and other objects are thrown about violently and the sidewall of the NASCAR stadium explodes. Tacea acts she grabs all the people that she can and moves them to the next state sparing them the death that was sure to claim them. She then returns to Housequake, just in time to see the being known as Omnipotus rise from the smoldering surface. Faceless motionless he stands waiting for Tacea.

"Behold this is when it gets good, he is why we are here you may have beaten us but that guy…well you'll see!" Pathogen adds.

"Well I hope you're up for this, that is who killed Relick. Which means he is damned tough to do that. Relick was the only one that could stand up to you when you went to Sky Hammer for the first time. If that's any indication of just how tough our boy was, they said he dropped Relick with one punch!" Housequake says while trying not to cough the Pathogen virus is spreading through his system despite his enchantments.

"Let's get you outta here before I clean this bastard's clock!" Tacea replies as she tries to move Quake.

"NO, you don't remove a warrior from the final battle when he still has life in him. That would be dishonorable, and that's not how I roll trust me I can still fight!" Housequake says.

"Alright well you need a soda and popcorn, 'cause this is gonna be a helluva fight here record it with my cell phone please!" Tacea replies as she stands ready, for what might be her final battle.

"Which button do I push? Oh, ok I got it to make me proud…for Relick and Shabazz, wait this won't be able to track your movements!" Housequake says loading the last chamber on his gun.

"You got it, boy!" Tacea replies as she seems to vibrate even faster, but she remains motionless staring down the neutralizer of nations as if they were in an old western.

"Make a move sweetie don't give him a chance damn it!" Housequake says as he looks at her, but her answer will shock him.

"We have made moves… a lot to make it more clear!" Tacea adds but never looks more serious or focused.

"What are you talking about girl I didn't see you move, I know you're fast but not that fast?" Housequake replies.

"We have both made over two-thousand strikes apiece, fighting test and he is good. Hold on to something, shield your eyes and ears, you're bout to feel the aftershock of our short double-dutch game!" Tacea says and with that small explosion happens all over the city, in the distance, and nearby. Chunks of earth sink like tons of weight had been dropped unseen leaving enormous impressions behind. Then comes the Ultra-sonic boom, incredible high winds are forcing visibility to become zero. Any glass or high-standing building shatters and falls in no particular order. For an unseen battle much was done before the eye could blink or thought given birth.

Omnipotus simply stands motionless as energy is surrounding him, but the same can be said about Tacea.

"GOTDAMN!" Is the only word Housequake can find?

"Sorry Quake this fight is beyond you I was designed to fight off a planet if need be, you won't be able to follow this battle. You won't even see me move from this spot it will be like I never left, if I move then that means that either that thing is dead or I'm dead! (She pulls out her cross and kisses it) Yo Omnipotus, Michael, or whatever you are…WAR WITH ME! Tacea yells, looking back at Quake one more time and then the battle begins anew!

Tacea makes the first move, in a time frame that we cannot fathom. She strikes the Archangel knocking him back; she then sweeps his leg, knocking him to the ground. She begins to strike him in every pressure point Shabazz taught her. It's a pity he has none.

"You like that, well you killed the friend that taught me that, and just like pizza I'm gonna be delivering you more in less than thirty minutes! 'Tacea says as Omnipotus is nowhere to be seen.

He manages to backhand, Tacea but she quickly responds as they trade blow for blow the city is being obliterated and Quake can only watch with the fallen horsemen at the destruction caused by the two Titans. Tacea remembers a thing and puts her thought into action, the battle has raged on in her timeline for weeks to us just mere seconds. Which, in the words of Bruce Lee, *"I want my fights over in seconds, not minutes!"* Make perfect sense to this point!

She grabs Iron chains, wraps them around her fists, and punches Omnipotus in the jaw repeatedly until he drops to one knee. She then binds his hands behind his back, the iron has cut his power so that he can't free himself. Tacea with the power of the Sky Hammer opens multiple portals and moves through each one to gather speed, and momentum that she could not achieve on our plane. She strikes the Archangel knocking him through one of the opened portals that she has created. To spare the planet the shock wave devastation she creates more portals as he flies through each one until his momentum is dissipated. He then lands back on earth with a thud that sinks the eastern seaboard; seemingly unconscious she drags him back to the original battle site with Housequake and the horsemen waiting.

"Ok, that's that let's take him to Warcast to figure the rest of this crap out. He was tough but I don't see how he took out Relick and Shabazz?" Tacea says.

"Well, I didn't even see your fight just explosions and these two idiots' mindless babble. They keep swearing that it's not over!" Housequake replies.

"It's not though you have great power, it's not enough to best Omnipotus!" Atrophy says.

"Really, 'cause he looks pretty out of it to me!" Tacea replies as she taps him with her foot assuring that he is out.

"You're just trying to hype 'em up, dumb ass just lay back, and shut up!" Tacea adds.

"Before we fade out, our work is done but you subdued him with mere iron chains for most supernatural chaps that would work. But in his case, you would need blessed iron and one other key element that I will not disclose. Our work here is done and so is your role in this game, I pity you for what comes next!" Atrophy says as he and Pathogen fade out.

Before Tacea can respond, Omnipotus is up and has slapped her in the center of her back as he begins to draw away the energy from the Sky Hammer stage she is currently in. She cannot move and the pain is unbearable, Quake fires his last round at the Arch Angel but to no effect. Tacea falls to the ground, as smoke flows from her body, she tries to transform but he has taken that ability away from her. Omnipotus raises his hand and in a blinding light Tacea is gone, only a smoking hole is left where she once was.

"TACEA, DAMN IT I'LL KILL YOU FOR THAT!" Housequake yells as the Arch Angel utters one word and the planet seems to shake!

"*WORTHY!*"

The same brilliant like that took Tacea has claimed Housequake!

Chapter 8

It's called a fist!

Darkness unfolds, and then suddenly an eruption of flame, the screams of people, and the decimation of life demons are running rampant clawing, tearing at the souls of the masses. Some visions of a Godless time surface anew, as our world is being destroyed utterly without hope. People try to flee to no avail as the madness of mankind has brought about damnation that will travel across the universe, obliterating all in its path. It is the end as the demons just feast on the will, but they notice something boiling in the fabric of their delightful hell. Something that scares even them and in one blinding flash, it is over. Again darkness is the maestro left without a band, and no one to give a concert to. Until a blue flash, and then red suddenly arrive making their way to the front of what was once our reality. They seem to give chase to one another, circling as if dancing. But dancing for whom, there is no one left anywhere to witness this montage of brilliance until violently they crash into one another, and out of the darkness comes a face without a face. It forces its way into my mind like the very first vision on my high school graduation night. I hear an incredibly scary roar, and then I awake.

"So it would seem that you are back amongst the living, so glad you could join us! 'Warcast says with his British accent.

"Oh man how long was I out, and what hit me?" Relick asks as he brings his feet to the floor.

"Well it's called a fist my good sir, and you've been down almost three and a half weeks. He broke every bone in your body and actually shut down your nervous system. The Gem of Destiny healed you but because of the substantial damage, it received in the battle went dark. You are quite lucky to be alive if it wasn't for Horus and Shabazz you wouldn't be here in the safe house I had for such an Omega-level event!" Warcast replies.

"Three…Wow, that archangel really knows how to party. Where is everyone and what the status of the world still shit I'm guessing, what am I saying of course it is!" Relick asks as he rubs both his hands against his face and head.

"Shabazz of course just left you about five minutes ago, and she been working on something that she's been apprehensive at best about sharing with anyone. Horus is trying to get information from your school colleagues; they've done quite an impressive job gathering info, and Mr. Rudolph Pettus left you a valuable video on the table to your right. They have discovered the whereabouts of important relics ancient that had helped other cultures, in our distant past survive the end times." Warcast says.

"Mr. Pettus, the man was always there when I needed him most wonder what words of wisdom he left on that recording, good old Al Hardy and Scott Hudson, they came through for me as always. Are they good where are they now? Relick asks.

"They did not survive, they, however, provide video feed storage deposits, so that we may locate these artifacts, it's taking Horus a bit of time trying to locate them, he was seriously injured trying to protect you. As it is, his power level has also been greatly diminished!" Warcast says.

"DAMN IT, I SHOULD have been there for them, I should have had their backs"! Relick yells trying to come to grips with all that has been lost.

"No my friend they knew the risks, and they made the ultimate sacrifice do not cheapen their part in this, for because of them we might have a bit of hope. But for more bad news…The Gem of Destiny has been damaged and fractured, Horus found you on the island of the Dominican Republic unconscious. You need to retrieve those fractured pieces and fuse them back into place. Make certain that whatever dirt, sand, or gravel, is also fused with it because they have absorbed the broken energy from the fractured pieces. The Gem is over there." Warcast says.

Relick staggers to it, shocked to see it damaged he didn't think it was possible to damage the gem.

"Omnipotus is vicious, he stopped me with one punch basically, split the Gem of Chaos all in a short battle, and cracked the Gem of Destiny damn!" Relick picks up the Gem of Destiny and it only flickers a bit before totally phasing out.

So he concentrates harder on the link he has with it, and it energizes but only at half-strength. Beside it is the Gem of Chaos pulsating ominously. He frowns at it and wants to destroy it.

"Don't even think about it you are going to need both to power the Armor of GOD, go check on Shabazz before you bloody do something stupid!" Warcast says.

"Yeah let me do just that, which room is she in?" Relick asks looking confused.

"Three doors down on your right the big one can't miss it." Warcast replies.

"Ok, got it!" Relick says.

He walks down the hall noticing all the fancy paintings and statues, he thinks to himself the man has taste. He can also hear music although it's low he tries to make out which tune it is, there is also a humming like electric machinery being used. From the third room, he notices a light blue glow also and as he enters there she is. As usual, working hard, she has on a tank top, spandex pants, and a tool belt; in her hands, she is using a welder. She looks strange with the welding helmet on, but she is totally focused, but now he can identify the tune. It is "Distant lover" by Marvin Gay

Watching her work as the sweat rolls off her arms and small of her back makes him a bit short of breath. She raises her helmet to get a better look at her work, and then her midsection comes into view. He begins to regret not getting closer to her and expressing more to her, and the song does not help him at all. She flows around the workshop like a sultry seductress. Then she removes the helmet, and belt then begins doing hanging sit-ups she has really begun to work up a sweat then jumps down with her back facing her unknown audience. Her curves and her incredibly defined backside are only enhanced as she pulls her pants up, Relicks mouth becomes increasingly dry only to have himself reduced to an action figure as she turns and begins grabbing her ankles stretching while standing. He can only watch as she reaches up towards the ceiling exposing a sweat-covered cleavage, he has had enough as he interrupts her session. He clears his throat and then speaks.

"What do you know about that song, are you kidding me?" Relick asks.

"OH MY GOD, YOU'RE UP?" Shabazz says, as she is overwhelmed with emotion as she runs to him grabbing him and tightly hugging him, she even goes so far as to lift him off his feet.

"Dang girl you been lifting, you act like I was dead or something put me down!" Relick says jokingly.

"I am so glad to see you moving you were down for so long!" Shabazz replies.

"Like I said what do you know about Marvin Gay?" Relick asks.

"Well I know the man was as bad-assed as they get, and it is so relaxing the music nowadays has no soul…No heart. Just weak wanna-be's making a lot of money to simply suck!" Shabazz says as she ties a shirt around her waist.

"Take it you saw me standing here right, neva could sneak up on you ever!" Relick asks as he rubs his face.

"Yep heard you as you stumbled down the hall, well somebody was, but then I could smell you, I know your scent! 'Shabazz says.

"What smell me?" Relick asks.

"Yep the ventilation is good here and I've only smelled you since kindergarten. Do you know what I would like to do? One last slow dance it's the end after all and my surprise is finished, so let's go you owe me!" Shabazz responds and extends her hand he accepts and they dance to the mighty sounds of Marvin.

"Everyone is gone the whole team and most of the population, almost like we are the last man and woman on the planet. We have these last few lasting moments, to hold each other you don't have to say anything just hold me close ok?" Shabazz says.

"I can do that, we have lost so much, I need to go see if my family is ok once I fix the gem. You have always been the bright spot in my life, I've never thanked you properly for being there always." Relick replies.

The two dance and its complete unison, like they've done this dance before a million times as they stare into each other's eyes Relick have a thought.

"Wait is this some kinda training session, I know you what's up girl!" Relick asks as their focus and breathing become intense.

"Yes it is, this allows you to concentrate on your foot movement and it's testing your neurological responses. Now, this next thing is going to be tricky it will test your heart." Shabazz says softly as she moves to kiss Relick.

She knows all too well that he was lost to her, and she does not want to waste this possibly final chance to show just how much she cares for him. Finally, he responds.

"Shabazz I…" Relick replies as she places her finger against his lips.

"Shhh…Just do what your heart wants complete this training!" Shabazz says as they tighten their embrace the feverish passion has been boiling over for years.

Suddenly Warcast blasts in shattering the moment of truth.

"Horus is back with the information…Wait have I stumbled upon some awkward moment what goes on here?" Warcast asks jokingly.

"Bro it was training, testing my motor reflex I've been out for a while…Footwork you know!" Relick replies trying to get his balance stabilized.

"INDEED!" Warcast says smiling.

Relick leaves and then goes to the main area, Warcast whispers to Shabazz.

"About bloody time, you two were killing me with your tip-toeing around love dance," Warcast says, as Shabazz only blushes and smiles as they go to join Relick.

"This is what your friends found and it is quite baffling as to how they found it, the human will never cease to amaze!" Horus says as he presents the video feed with invaluable information on it.

But before the information is played Warcast shows the remaining members what has happened to the world. Noting how Omnipotus has entered the Pacific Ocean reached the bottom and back to the surface in a blink. Then you see many U.S.O's trying to flee the planet but he zaps them all as hundreds of aliens are disintegrated like bugs on a zapper trap. Then the majority of the world is shown in ruins, none shall escape this well-deserved Rapture.

"This my friends, is what we are facing, if this information that your friends have found is fruitful then a chance we might have," Warcast says as he prepares the Intel.

"GOD is truly angry with us all, human and non-human. We so messed up… we could have fixed this just a bit more kindness and respect for life and each other." Relick replies as heads are lowered in shame at humanity.

"He is quite past the point of petty anger, he is livid every place seems to be burning!" Warcast replies.

"I don't see any animals, just dead things and people suffering, how can there still be so many demons left?" Relick adds as the mystic monitors continue to show the cataclysm around the globe.

"I will now provide a brief rundown of the history of the Armor of GOD and the Akashic Records." Warcast waves his hand and the room is filled with images of Africa and Egypt's distant and troubled past. They too faced a similar threat to all they held dear. I will let the spell narrate the story if you don't mind?" Warcast says as a disembodied voice begins to narrate.

In the Sands of Sudan around 2,500 B.C., there was a Nubian ethnicity called Kushites, the Kushites were building a civilization equal to their Egyptian neighbors, they were doing this at the same time the British were building Stonehenge, and the Egyptians started building their first pyramids. They had developed some of the first brick designs as well as a strong, literature, art, mathematical, and social base; they were fierce powerful wrestlers, proficient in hand-to-hand combat, and incredibly deadly archers. But they had two rare commodities gold and an even rarer metal Nubium the strongest metal known, supposedly gifted from the God "Amun"(Fallen angel). The black metal was used in much of their weaponry, sword edges, and arrow tips, it was made and fashioned by a mystical Kushite "Smitty" he was the only one that Amun provided knowledge on how to shape the virtually indestructible metal. The metal when fashioned into weaponry could penetrate any shield or armor. The Egyptians were content with the Kushites as long as they traded gold with them and had virtually no knowledge of the metal Nubium, but the Pharaoh Tutmou the 1st around 1,500 B.C. decided he wanted the gold and to enslave the people they had been at peace with all those centuries. So he launched a sneak attack on Kerma. Kerma was a vastly important trading post by way of the Nile, during a trade for ebony, ivory, and gold they overwhelmed their unsuspecting neighbors. They sacked the region enslaved and usurped the gold but could find no trace of the Nubium as they tortured the mystic Smitty

"Kusfabar" he would not tell them. Kusfabar was allowed to live in hopes that he would divulge the whereabouts of the precious metal. It was hidden in a Deffufa, which means "Brick Monolith" it stands in the ancient town of Kerma making it one of the oldest buildings in the world. The Kushites in order to survive had to adopt the teachings of their Egyptian conquers. 700 B.C. 800 years after their invasion Egypt had withdrawn from Kush a more pressing issue had arisen, an ancient evil Libyan powerful demon king called "Bulgaro" had set out to conquer and wipe out the Egyptians and the "Temple of Amun." The Egyptians sought out the most unlikely of help, the once conquered Kushites, they asked the Kushite warrior Piankhy. The god Amun instructed Kusfabar to build "The Armor of God" he did just that the armor was powered by two incredibly powerful gems. The armor was presented to Piankhy and he launched the campaign to take back Egypt with a massive army filled with the best archers and hand-to-hand combatants. After a ferocious battle with the demon king Bulgaro, Piankhy broke the neck of the demon and tore his brain from his skull. Freeing Egypt and saving the known world at the time, Piankhy and his followers became Egypt's 25th dynasty. Piankhy was given two crowns red and white symbolizing the rule of upper and lower Egypt. After a while, Piankhy gave the throne over to his brother Shabaka, but he placed The Armor of God away in the temple of Jebel Barka along with the Akashic records, for the need for such power was over. The two warrior kings fought Egypt's foes for numerous successful campaigns, and around 700 B.C. Taharqs the descendant of Shabaka even saved Jerusalem and King Solomon's temple from an assault by the Assyrians this act of heroism was even noted in the old testament by Hebrew theologians, but the Assyrians had other ideas. They had been defeated in the past and had heard of weakness in the rule of Taharqs. The Kushites had a claim to both upper and lower Egypt in 593 B.C. Egyptian, now with a new army and renewed rage, the Assyrian leader Psamtik led an army to control Egypt rolling the Kushite's borders back to Thebes. Egypt was retaken and thus brought the reign of the Kushites came to an end. Psamtik even went so as far as to try and wipe out any traces that the 25th dynasty of Egypt ever had existed. Psamtik's grandfather was put to death by a Kushite unknown leader. Smashing statues and even the Cobras off the crowns of such said statues, Cobras were considered sacred, and this was considered sacrilegious. Up to this point, the legend of the Kushites began to grow. In the 1930s an explorer seeking glory and fame named George Reisner. He had heard about great power and treasure from the legendary Nubian ethnicity called the "Kush" they were equal in power and on par with their Egyptian neighbors for a time they were civil towards one another as the story goes they had built great temples and monuments that resembled their Egyptian neighbors. Reisner was in awe at the ancient and fascinating hieroglyphs, in the halls of the Kushite temples and refused to believe that a Nubian ethnicity could build such a complex, educated, and prosperous civilization. Because of his fascist and superior American mentality, it began to cripple his mind, and judgment of his soul became tainted he was quoted as saying. "Its very race seems to be a product of its poverty and isolation, a negroed Egyptian mixture fused together on a river bank. Too far away, too poor to attract a stronger or better race!" This line of impure thinking led the forces of good to collapse the ceiling killing several of his diggers thus almost bankrupt he had to leave his search for power. His records were taken away by some of his hired African workers after the collapse a massive sandstorm raged covering the findings and they sold them to an ancient art dealer in western Africa. The records had never been found until now.

"This is what your mates have uncovered," Warcast says as he plays the podcast from the Hardy and Hudson expedition.

"Hey, Yorel uh I believe we have found the things you have been looking for," Al says as he adjusts the camera for a clear and better angle.

"It is really creepy here, glad that Al packed these weapons the crew even feels a bit more secure even though some won't go any further!" Scott adds.

"The Hieroglyphics read like a road map, the chamber or room is right there our team is setting up lights now," Al says as they enter the room, Scott follows down the wide corridor leading to the room.

"There are two doors here…but the Hieroglyphics stop Scott whatcha got?" Al asks.

"I don't know but it seems as though we are not alone the men won't come in this room, it's cursed they keep saying," Scott replies, as they hear disembodied screeching from seemingly every direction. The movement comes from every direction but they can't follow the movements. They ready their weapons.

"If we don't make it, we have provided this Intel to be live fed back base camp, but this is it you can feel the energy. The only part that isn't favored here is the telling sign look for the gold flashing on a large rock pillar, it will point the rest of the way!" Al says as he yells to Scott to look out.

"AL ON YOUR LEFT, KILL IT!" Scott yells as they fight violently against the quick-moving assault of untrackable killers.

They watch, as the rest of the team is eviscerated, and the two fight valiantly. The camera then is knocked over and the room is filled with smoke, dust, and the screams of the expedition. The last image seen is a partial face and an eye of something that is inhuman.

"That is all that we have, we know the approximate location of our targets, thanks to those two great friends of yours they have shown tremendous support in what we are trying to accomplish. Their loss is terrible, to say the least so something there did not want them to find what they did." Warcast says to the rest of the group, which has become very sad and focused on the task at hand.

"So the gems are not at full power because one is still missing fragments, that need to be put back right?" Relick asks as he places his hand across his heart uttering a small prayer for his friends quietly.

"Yes, I will get you there and then we must go quickly to Africa we don't have much time left, but I still believe that we can get the attention of the creator. Mercy may yet still be part of the universe!" Horus says.

"We still gotta make that stop in the Dominican Republic you said that's where the fragments of the gems are located. Let's go Shabazz time won't wait! Relick says.

"You two go ahead I'll catch you in Africa, there are a few finishing touches that I have to make on my little project. It seems that Omnipotus removed my "Fists of Destiny ability, it was like he just siphoned off the energy. Haven't been able to activate it since the battle." Shabazz replies as she walks in the direction of her workshop.

"So he just has no weakness, I sure hope they know what we are doing personally I just want a rematch and hit 'em as hard and fast as I can," Relick says.

"Be careful what you face is what we've been defending you from most of your life, it is the Mabus translated means the Anti-Christ this is his time and I know that he has wanted The Armor of God more than anything to battle and kill Michael or Omnipotus. The energy released has given the location of the armor and I fear that he is already there, however he cannot activate it without a true human vessel. Man when I tell you that you need to be on your guard, I mean it in the most profound way he will try and twist you!" Shabazz says as she walks away and continues tightening bolts and screws on her covered project.

"Ok well hurry up, seems as though we won't be able to do this thing without you!" Relick responds walking away.

"Since when have you ever been able to do anything without me, like this is anything new, just don't forget what I taught you?" Shabazz says jokingly giving Relick pause before he continues to Horus and Warcast he simply shakes his head and smiles.

"Are you ready, time is important the very ones that pray have been directed to myself and the remaining light mages. They are all that have kept this world from falling; their very energy has been tied in a knot here and at other key points on the planet. But the threads of faith, and hope are breaking!" Warcast says as he motions his hands reinforcing with divine energy the rapidly snapping bands of hopeful energy.

"Horus you ready?" Relick asks.

"Of course I am, we are off!" Horus replies as the room lights up and in a flash, Relick and Horus are gone.

Warcast stands on one leg before raising the other one and levitates with legs crossed Indian style. He begins to talk out loud as he hovers above the marked floor.

"I have sent my final friends to their doom, how will they accomplish this goal? I fear this task for mere mortals has its limits!" Warcast says as a bluish light fills the room accompanied by a voice followed by a form. It is the spirit of Merlin.

"So the end times are here once again, you cannot lose hope until hope is lost. I see that your comrades have buckets of hope left, his nature, his task; his birthright is to make a change if the strength is within him. Vexed or not this mortal will not be so easily beaten, the Light Lords chose wisely." Merlin says as a shocked look takes the face of Warcast.

"How…Are you truly here to share the wisdom I never thought that I would ever see you, not on this plane of reality? As you speak I am truly humbled, but is there a chance for this turn about in the favor of the righteous few?" Warcast asks while breaking his hovering mode to engage Merlin in conversation person to person for this is an extremely rare chance. After all, he is the last of Merlin's bloodline.

"Indeed there is, indeed there is allow me to show you one of the groups of our past that created humans, they were the hand that designed the DNA for early Europeans spurring our evolution between 3,000 and 6,000 years ago. Yes, they played GOD, behold the beings responsible for our very existence here at the end of all things now you have the truth!" Merlin responds as he places a phantom hand on the shoulder of Warcast, Warcast is left speechless as he looks on at his creators and vanishes with the spirit of Merlin.

Chapter 9

Sudan, Africa Horus has teleported the two to the location of the Armor of God, and the Akashic Records.

"This place is really impressive, the sands tell an entirely different silent tells of the history of the world," Relick says as he picks up sand and watches it run through his hand.

"Yes civilization started right here on this continent, you should have seen it from the beginning mankind staggering around trying to find meaning in this new world. But over there see that flashing light on that rock formation, just like Warcast said.

That is where we will find the Armor of God, and possibly find favor in his eyes?" Horus responds standing proud.

They are at Temple of Jebel Barka, where Relick's friend's last stand was, it is evident because a small camp still remains though it's in ruins, and all vehicles are totaled. Coming in the distance are figures that slowly take the shape of humans, entering the ruined temples.

"Man, who do you think they are, they don't look friendly?" Relick asks.

"They are not the enemy I feel that they arrived too late to help your friends, they are the sworn Disciples of Saint Maurice. They are in possession of supernatural weapons blessed by Saint Maurice and passed down through the generations, that have held demons and evil creatures at bay, for centuries. Saint Maurice (the First Black saint) was killed in 287 A.D. when he and his followers refused to forsake Christ and he was one of the last known people to hold the Spear of Christ 286 A.D. Even though he fought in the Roman (Theban) Legion he and his 6,600 men were killed in the military punishment known as decimation. This was the punishment he and his men received for not attacking Christians at the command of the Roman Empire. His place in the afterlife is assured, for in life he and his troops were devoted and fierce warriors." Horus says as the men come closer.

"Yeah Al, and Scott could have used them or us!" Relick replies as he looks towards the entrance of the temple becoming angry.

"They are warriors from all parts of the continent, but primarily made up of the Zulu," Horus says, as the warriors stop before him and all take a knee.

"Lord Horus have we arrived too late, we were alerted to the presence of evil but then it stopped?" A Nubian warrior asks still down on one knee, clutching a spear in one hand.

"They know who you are, wow guess you are pretty famous who would have thought?" Relick asks.

"I know my true identity I am one of the few fallen angels that have knowledge of my origins I have shared this information with them from the beginning," Horus replies, about 30 warriors all standing in unison as Horus raises his hand and directs the next order of business.

"You warriors stand guard out here if anything that is not us, KILL IT!" Horus says.

"As you wish Lord Horus, men to your positions!" The Nubian leader commands as the men take an impressive formation around the front of the temple.

"Are you ready Relick, Mabus awaits!" Horus asks.

"Born that way, let's do this!" Relick responds as they enter the glowing entrance and disappear from sight. The passage way is dark and long Horus lights the torches that are along the walls of the passage giving them light.

Then they come to the fallen bodies of Relick's friends, the room is huge and seemingly has no sides but suspended in the air is the Armor of God, and on a stone slab the Akashic records. But they are not alone, out of a dark corner comes a sinister voice.

"Behold the pale horse, and the guests of honor have finally decided to join us?" Mabus says, with pale white skin, and blue veins bulging from all over his body. And burning sky blue eyes, with a cloak and drapes that seem to float around his body.

"So I take it you are Mabus, man you cats get uglier and uglier?" Relick replies.

"Ouch, such harsh words I come bearing gifts I offer you a chance for survival!" Mabus says.

"Well, I really don't see how you can offer anything, being that you are the Anti-Christ you've been waiting for this opportunity for a grip!" Relick says.

"So you walk in with this worthless fallen angel, and I'm the enemy? Do you know what you have to do to get kicked out of heaven, tisk, tisk it's pretty bad. What... you didn't know from the look on your face he didn't tell you did he? Didn't you tell him Zotheal, that's his real name before he was expelled from heaven!" Mabus says trying to divide the two.

"It does not matter what was, what matters is what is. I have paid for those crimes and I will never betray my father if given the chance and if he does not grant me the chance so be it. I made a bad choice that I will have to live with, he has rules!" Horus replies proudly.

"Just want you to know that has nothing to do with me and you so step aside while I collect those!" Relick says as the gems leave his pockets and hover above his head.

Mabus looks and is attempting to mentally pull them towards him, the destiny gem stays fixed but the chaos gem shakes as if it wants to join him, but then Mabus releases his mental attempt neither gem will join him.

"Those gems are so powerful if you only knew, together they would allow you to conquer all. You wouldn't need the Armor of Blah, his name sickens me but he would see your world and everyone destroyed, he knew this was coming. That humanity was incapable of honoring him or anything, but he allowed you to exist how is this fair, for you to have the weight of the Cosmoverse resting on your shoulders!" Mabus says as he moves closer.

"So I guess this is the point where you try to turn me right, I see how you keep scoping the gems not gonna happen brah! Relick replies as he prepares for battle.

"I don't deny that I have always coveted those gems, there are so many weapons of power in the universe but those things are like hot sauce on a tamale. What I offer you is knowledge and a different way out of this together because if you fail we all die. Horus I see you stay where you are I sense that you are not as strong as normal the battle with Omnipotus has really been hard on you, glad I brought back up BOLTHAG come!" Mabus summons his warrior general and his minions, he is an African Popobawa a vicious one-eyed bat-like creature that lives in the dense jungles and sands of Africa. He also has an Impundulu at his command a huge lighting bird of legend to join the stand off. Both creatures have been devouring man since the dawn of life.

"Are these abominations supposed to scare me, because make no mistake I am still more powerful than you can see?" Horus asks.

"We won't stop until we get what we came for, hope we can kill you in the process?" Relick says.

"We, with the Armor of Blah and the gems, could crush Omnipotus, lives could be saved on countless levels, You have always felt something was wrong with the world, even before you had the gem, you would have nightmares, see demons and all that is happening now, I offer you a chance to make the difference that you thought you could but really change it all. See I can't touch the Armor of Blah or the gems but you can, together we can stop all of this and save every single person you love or care about!" Mabus replies as he postures with his minions.

"So you're saying that this could be ended if I go against God that things would go back to the original ways?" Relick asks as he glances at Horus.

"Not you, me, I have no love for him, I just know what he has done to my kind. If I could just borrow your body for an hour or two I promise to give it back, slightly banged up, but you'll have it back scouts honor!" Mabus says as he makes an X across where his heart should be.

Relick looks at Horus as more of the one-eyed bat-like creatures crawl from the darkness.

"Are you up for this, you seem pretty weak" Relick asks.

"Horus as well as I can be, to the death!" Horus replies.

"Whoa, don't be going all death seeker on me now we got this!" Relick says quietly.

"He's already dead his life-force draining, he can't help you any more but I on the other hand can. Let's end all this madness, save the cosmos and all that!" Mabus says as he extends his hand to Relick, and the creatures begin to surround them.

"So you can't use the gems or the armor without me a willing one of chosen, looks like you have a big problem dog!" Relick says as he grabs Mabus by the hand and knocks him into the air with a vicious upper cut.

"You won't be able to use the gems, this will be a fight based on your skills and determination!" Horus explains as he tackles the leader Popobawa.

The other creatures attack and the battle begins, the Impundulu strikes Horus in the back with mystic lightening. Stunning him momentarily, in a blink, Horus transforms into his Falcon form. He begins spinning like a jigsaw blade and cuts one of the Impundulu's leg's off. Mabus begins to float towards Relick seemingly unaffected by the previous attack.

"So that is your choice? You know a dead body is just as good, I think well we can put it to the test shall we play for keeps?" Mabus asks as the temple begins to vibrate.

"That's the only way I know how to play!" I sure hope that I remember what Shabazz had taught me! Relick says as he takes a deep breath.

The two trade punches neither getting any leverage on the other, but Relick takes Mabus to the ground and begins to systematically punish him with crushing elbows to the face, and clavicle and there is a thunderous crack as if the breaking of a bone.

"Did I break something, let me see if I can wreck something else?" Relick adds.

As soon as Relick attempts to make a new move, Mabus hits him with energy in the abdomen knocking him back. Several of the one-eyed creatures swarm Relick as they have Horus. The two battle savagely killing many of the creatures but the creatures will not stop their attacks. The Impundulu though severely injured fires his deadly lighting at Relick but Horus jumps in front of the blast intended for Relick and is brought down hard.

"Horus I got you, buddy, come on man I can't do this alone!" Relick says.

"I believe my friend you are going to have to, that was a powerful burst you must take the creature down now!" Horus replies as he tries to gain his remaining power.

"I'm on it you just hold on!" Relick says as he fires his most powerful energy bolt, causing the Impundulu to explode.

The creature screeches in pain as it is no more, Popobawa and his dark comrades attack Relick, and then Mabus joins to quickly put an end to the fight.

"It won't be long now boy, you are outnumbered, overpowered and you don't have your gems or the armor to help you. WHAT WILL YOU DO…DIE!" Mabus screams.

Relick is fighting the beasts with everything he has, and suddenly there is an explosion that opens the ceiling. An object falls through the opening when the smoke clears it is a Robotic form clad in purple and gold. Its operator is none other than the mighty Shabazz.

"Sorry it took me so long I had to add a few more touches!" Shabazz says as she exposes the armaments on the battle suit and they are impressive.

"Glad you could join us, glad you brought that. Well Shabazz you know the saying?

WAR WITH ME! Relick yells as he rips arms and legs off the creatures beating them and impaling them with their own appendages.

"I thought you'd never ask!" Shabazz says she unloads with heavy rounds and energy weapons. She then begins battling with the combat moves she is famous for.

"NO, NO, NO DAMN YOU, YOU ARE NOT PART OF THIS EQUATION. SO YOU ARE THE MEDDLESOME SHABAZZ I HEAR SO MUCH ABOUT?" Mabus asks.

"Yep but I believe you won't be hearing anything for awhile, Relick cover your ears!" Shabazz says as she fires a high-pitched blast that brings the whole lot to their knees.

A creature tries to grab Shabazz she quickly reacts by grabbing it out of the air, and filling its face with high-piercing rounds until its face looks like ground beef. She throws the mangled carcass to the feet of Mabus. Distracted Relick renews his assault on Mabus smashing him all around the room, while Shabazz makes short work of the creatures.

"You thought this was gonna be easy, that I would just give into your dumbass rant? Come on now I have heard better, you know damn well you don't want to save the world. You want to run it and everything else, not gonna happen!" Relick says.

"Well it was worth a shot, but this is far from over you are my objective, and I will not be denied these weapons that will allow me to dominate all!" Mabus replies as he takes Relick by the arms and slings him through a pillar and wall.

Mabus then attacks Relick with Hellfire while he is momentarily stunned, its effect is brutal as it not only burns the flesh, but the mind, and soul. Relick grunts, and then Mabus is on him beating him like a rabid dog. Covered in dust and sand Relick feels fingers around his throat as Mabus begins to choke him. Mabus smears tainted sand into the face and eyes of Relick, causing him tremendous pain and he begins to lose sight.

"You will have nothing this day after I am done with you, I offered you a chance to save everyone, family, friends all that you hold dear. You just had to be a Jackass and try to deny me… the Anti-Christ my right to rule. I will remove your soul from this body and TAKE IT ALL!" Mabus says as he continues to apply pressure to the throat of Relick.

Relick brings out the Waters of Tomas and pours it into the hands of Mabus. Mabus releases him in pain, as Relick then splashes a huge amount of the water into the eyes of Mabus. Mabus grabs his face in agony, he stands and all that can be heard is the splitting of air as Shabazz takes his head with her Noir Blade. His body drops to its knees lifeless. The remaining creatures see this and they flee, Horus comes to his feet to join the others.

"I see you haven't lost your dramatic side, that was a sweet move!" Relick says.

"He had it coming and he really talks too much," Shabazz replies.

"It is not over, he is transforming he has one last gambit!" Horus says in a weakened voice.

The body of Mabus begins to flop violently and grows; he begins to sprout multiple snake-like heads. Huge wings break through his back; his body becomes covered in white and gray scales. His arms and legs become muscular and massive, and clawed hands and feet become prominent as he becomes a more formidable foe.

The gems both streak to the side of Relick as if ready for battle, and The Armor of God begins to glow as two fixtures open on the armor seemingly the perfect fit for the gems to be used as power sources.

"You must get the armor to remember Revelations in the bible. This is the seven-headed dragon that devours all you must kill him myself and Shabazz will buy you the time you need!" Horus says and he seems to be rejuvenated.

"Why are the gems responding now, they wouldn't budge at first!" Relick asks as the dragon-headed Mabus begins to complete his transformation.

"He changed the rules once he transformed, he was beaten and the gems only remained neutral as it was a test of your resolve. Now they will assist you in fighting him!" Shabazz replies still clad in the battle mech.

Horus plows into Mabus hard knocking him down; he then grabs him by the leg and drags him through the temple causing untold damage until he throws him outside. Skipping across the sand, he follows quickly to engage him further as the Zulu warriors engage Mabus also.

"Place the gems before the armor, they will do the rest. Make it fast don't know how long we can hold Mabus!" Shabazz says as she streaks out to battle.

Relick quickly moves toward the armor, he places the gems into the slots and stands back. The armor floats and fuses to Relicks skin, he feels power coursing through his body he is then joined by the spirit of Saint Maurice. The spirit of Saint Maurice begins to explain, what is at hand and offers another gift to aid in the battle.

"This is the Spear of Destiny, everything else you have seen has been a forgery. I entrust this to you along with the Akashic records, these will help you with the final battles that you now face. Make sure if you are successful here that you go to your family home and make peace. It is on the 37-degree parallel a lay line that has enormous magical energy that will enhance you further!" The spirit of Maurice says as he hands Relick the Spear of Destiny.

The spear is held sideways as Relick reaches for it, the spear flips around the room and then to the back of the Armor of GOD which now is a part of Relicks costume. Relick is silent as he ponders what the spirit of Saint Maurice has said, Saint Maurice then smiles at Relick and points to the battle outside. He then places one fist across his chest and vanishes. Relick knows what must be done now; he mentally changes the GOD armor back to his original costume and keeps the spear and book handy. Outside Shabazz and Horus are locked in battle with Mabus he is completely transformed into seven dragon heads, each equipped with its own special power, Earth, Wind, Fire, Water, Ice, Lightening, Acid, and Gravity his body has grown to thirty feet. Horus lights into Mabus staggering him and the Nubian warriors attack also injuring Mabus with their divine weapons, but the powers of Mabus begin to take them down as they fight valiantly. Shabazz streaks in unloading a barrage of artillery that allows the warriors to take cover, Horus punches the middle dragon's head off Mabus knocking him down but is sprayed with hellish acid that corrodes his body again diminishing his power and life-force he is hit with a gravity surge that puts him down into the sand. Unable to move Mabus fires ice immobilizing Horus, as he moves in for the kill Shabazz impales him with a holy Javelin, that sends him screaming he tries to re-treat but Shabazz fills his right-wing full of holes causing him to crash headfirst into the desert sand.

"Horus you must stand I do not believe Relick is ready yet?" Shabazz says as she helps him up.

The head that Horus removed from Mabus is now growing back, and it strikes hitting Shabazz's robot armor with the hell acid and hellfire. It damages her armor to the point of ejection; the armor is about to explode Horus propels it towards Mabus as a bomb. Mabus does not flinch but powers up to use all dragonhead abilities to finish Shabazz and Horus. The Nubian Warriors all gather with their mystical war shields in front of Shabazz and the injured Horus, in unison, slam their shields into the sand surface. A protective barrier is activated, as Mabus fires all dragonhead powers at the barricade, the warriors are sent flying and scattered. Either they are burned to death, dissolved in the acid, sandblasted, electrocuted, or sent screaming into orbit, they made the ultimate sacrifice.

"NOOOOO!" Horus screams as he watches in horror.

"It's your turn now, say hello to your maker for me and let him know we shall meet really soon!" Mabus says as he powers up for a final attack.

Mabus fires all energy blasts at the defenseless heroes, Relick streaks just in time, as the energy was about to strike. He puts up his force field amplified by the Armor of GOD; although it's not fully activated it still provides immense protection. It absorbs the energy and Relick sends it right back at Mabus, by a factor of ten. Mabus screams and falls from the sky, burning from the attack Mabus rushes the warriors. Relick activates the Spear of Destiny it extends and vibrates with gargantuan power; Relick takes flight and beheads three of the dragonheads. They this time do not regenerate; the stumps that once held their heads have been cauterized. Mabus is forced down on all fours because of the pain and shock.

"This was not to be, not the end that I had foreseen!" Mabus says.

"Well I tell you what, it is what I had foreseen another big mouth liar, demon thing getting its ass kicked…BY A LOWLY HUMAN WITH FAITH!" Relick yells.

Relick then flies straight into the body of Mabus from overhead and explodes spear first from the chest of Mabus. It is over the battle with the Anti-Christ is over, his body lays lifeless on the smoldering desert surface. Relick retracts the Destiny Spear and places it on his back it magically snaps into place. Suddenly Relick gets a familiar eerie feeling, as the words rip through the air. "WORTHY" Relick streaks quickly to Shabazz and Horus only to see a flash and Horus is no more, he has been judged.

"NO DAMN IT JUST TAKING EVERYTHING I CARE ABOUT, OMNIPOTUS I'M COMING FOR YOU ONE WAY OR THE OTHER

WE FINISH THIS!" Relick yells as Shabazz says a prayer on one knee for the fallen. Horus who has been with them from the beginning is now no more.

"Then that's it, then only three of us left I've heard that word more than once. Each time I've heard it someone on the battlefield vanishes!" Shabazz replies.

"It's like he takes them, I don't understand why but I have to let Warcast know that we have the weapons. Warcast we have the Relics, do you copy?" Relick asks as he tries to raise Warcast on their earpiece communication links.

"I believe that we are all that's left of the Celestial Seven!" Shabazz says calmly.

Relick pauses for a moment and continues to try and reach Warcast, he repeats over and over but only silence responds. Then the wind begins to blow across the desert and the two prepare for the final showdown. Relick remembers the words of Saint Maurice go home and make peace with your family.

Chapter 10

Home

The drive was long and quiet until Relick shares thoughts and fears beyond what he will be facing. Even the end of the world pales in comparison to what evil has done and his family has allowed to happen. The rift is beyond repair, but at the end of all things, he is here at the advice of a Saint to try and salvage…HOPE!

"You know we're broken?" Relick asks.

"Yeah but we now have a fighting chance," Shabazz says.

"No I mean my family, Osiris really did a number on us!" Relick replies.

"You guy's have been broken, your family was cursed, targeted to fail. The design was to wipe out your bloodline to stop your hand in all this." Shabazz says.

"I've watched my brothers and sister's marriages fail, lose connection with their kids. Even seen their divorces go so bad, that the exes change the male children's name back to the name of the mother wiping out our name and legacy. My brother never even put up a fight, while the other one you know which one. Turns to the bottle trying to find GOD at the bottom of it. All he's found is a place to try and bury his shame and shadiness." Relick responds.

"I remember being there as kids, well you were a kid I was well into my hundreds. But I never could understand your mother, while I did have insight into your family history she was never clear to me?" Shabazz responds.

"I never really felt family ties except to my sister Shante, I remember when there was no food at home. There were times when my mother wouldn't give me food; she made sure that she had food and stuff for the new husband but none for me. I remember you always had food for me, taking it from your freezer and sneaking it to me. Those days or nights when my mother would have a flashback of my father and would raise a hand to hit me. Hell, I didn't even do anything wrong, those cold winter nights when I would sleep in my car once I could finally afford one in the dead of winter she just didn't want me there. The windows would freeze over then, there you were scraping ice off the windows and staying the night with me, I miss that 83 civic." Relick says.

"But yet you still remained true of heart, and never gave in to all the evil and turmoil that you constantly faced. You could have given in and made excuses like so many do but you dug your heels deep and became a respectable man. You don't drink, smoke, do drugs, never been to jail finished school, and you have no kids out of wedlock. That is saying a lot and is much to be proud of!" Shabazz responds.

"Without your kindness, and support where would I have been so many times I wanted to give up, and just go anywhere, anywhere that I was known times that I just didn't care! If I never have before I wanna thank you, for everything." Relick answers as he grips the steering wheel.

They pass signs letting them know that they are about to enter his town, the neighborhood is run down people move about slowly like zombies, with broken buildings and windows smashed. The sky seems to burn like fire but in the distance, in the direction of his home the sky is clear like the eye of a Hurricane has settled over it. He pulls up to his street and notices that his street seems untouched by all the outside forces, the end of the world does not yet know his birth home. Kids are playing in the street, as cars can hardly get through and the parents look on saying nothing, even here at the judgment and the end of all things. His family has gathered well most of them for a long traditional family function. Good food and good music. But he can feel the end coming so he must make whatever peace with those he can.

He comes to see his deranged brother, and sister that loves drama he can't locate his niece, older sister, and eldest brother. The most shocking thing is his parents are talking but it seems to be intense, and soon turns into a shouting match.

"Well, now that's a sight I never thought that I'd live, to see my parents, talking!" Relick says, as his eyes are open wide.

"I haven't seen those two together since we were in elementary school, this can't be good and they don't seem to be enjoying each other given the body language!" Shabazz responds.

"Well look what crawled out of the litter box, why the hell are you here you ain't been around in years? Amire you looking good girl, why are you still hanging around this chump?" His brother asks clearly a bit intoxicated, barely able to hold on to his glass trying to look cool.

"You know what they say, one man's opinion can be another man's Emancipation. Your little brother ain't so bad, he's an honorable and good man!" Shabazz replies while giving Relick a wink.

"Hmp if you say so, he just acts like a cat that thinks he is all high and mighty in my eyes!" The brother responds trying to get a rise out of Relick.

"Let me tell you something fool if I hadn't stayed away you see those two over there? They would be mourning the loss of a child, best thing you can do is keep your mouth and stupid drunk words off me. I didn't come here for all that, yak, yak you speaking!" Relick says while trying not to punch a hole in his wretched brother's shirt.

His drama-filled sister then enters the conversation, placing her opinion where it doesn't belong.

"Well why did you come, we are so good without you coming around nobody misses your combative presence!" Sister says taking the side of the drunken brother.

"You need to just stay out of it, it's between those two. You always put your nose where it doesn't belong just like you did with my daughter. We don't even have a relationship because you running around acting like she is your child, with your poisonous lies!" His sister Shante says.

"Well if you had been a better mother and not laid all the responsibility on our mama then you would have your daughter. She had her more than you did, can't nobody help that you gave her a sorry-ass father you're just crazy! The sister responds.

"Bitch I know you ain't tripping you're still mad because you lost your baby, you with your messy ass ways ain't nothing gonna live in your dirty womb! GET YOUR BARREN ASS OUTTA MY FACE GIRL BEFORE I FUCK YOU UP!? Shante says as they approach as if to fight.

The opening in the clear sky seems to be closing with each hate-spat word, and Relick and Shabazz notice that demons have begun to show up unnoticed by his family. As if they are waiting for the final bond to break, as it seems they won't have to wait long. Relick stands between the two sisters holding them back before they come to blows. When his drunk brother makes a huge mistake.

"Stop ya'll please we are at the end of the world, don't do this!" Relick begs.

"GET YOUR ASS OUTTA HERE DON'T COME AROUND HERE NOW ACTING LIKE SOME RIGHTEOUS GOTDAMN PEACEMAKER! His drunken brother says and shoves Relick into the grill and food table, Relick is enraged.

Relick is slow to get up not realizing that his hand is still in the grill fire, he only has one thing on his mind snatching the skin off his brother. His brother takes a combative stance taunting him to fight. Relick is all but happy to give him one, no matter what the cost might be.

"Come on punk let's settle this thing once and for all, the theme of today is Big brother slaps lil brother!" The brother says.

"BOY I TRIED TO SPARE THE FAMILY THIS, BUT YOU JUST BOUGHT A ONE-WAY TICKET TO THE TOWN OF ASS KICKED, POPULATION YOU!" Relick replies and in one push sends his brother flying across the yard, smashing the picnic table and finally getting tangled up into the Volleyball net.

But Relick is not done yet; quickly he grabs his brother from his entanglement and throws him to the ground still holding him by the throat. Shabazz rushes in to stop Relick from killing him.

"STOP YOREL, YOU'RE GOING TO KILL HIM LET HIM GO PLEASE, WE NEED TO LEAVE!" Shabazz says as she grabs the arm of Relick.

His brother's eyes begin to roll to the back of his head as Relick has slowly applied pressure to his neck. He sees this and stops not because he deserves it, but because his mother would just see him as a complete mistake. Relick punches a hole next to his brother's head, and then slowly releases him.

"I should have taken your head off, after all the shit you've pulled WE ARE DONE FOR GOOD!" Relick says.

"Get off him you make me sick why are you here, just leave you always mess stuff up!" His messy sister says as she pushes him.

"Don't push him like that, you saw he started it and hit Yorel first!" Shante replies.

"Kick dirt in the hole so that they won't notice it!" Shabazz whispers to Relick, he does, and then his mother and father approach.

His mother begins slapping and pushing Relick screaming at the top of her lungs. The surrounding demons gather closer and begin to smile as his mother assaults him. Relick tries to cover up for some odd reason his mother's blows actually hurt him. Shabazz twitches but stands her ground watching for a moment then she drops her head in shame.

"All you ever do is come around worthless, and unwanted who do you think you are!?" His mother says still hitting him until his father grabs her.

"Again I haven't done anything wrong, again you humble, and demoralize me I get attacked and you beat me. I don't understand this family, why is it always me?" Relick asks.

"Woman have you lost your mind why are you attacking him, I came here to make peace and clear the air but you have gone too far!" His father says while restraining his mother.

"Too far, no let me tell him the truth then!" His mother says.

"Don't do this let it be!" His father replies.

"Here is the truth, you are a mistake well not really. You were something I put together to make sure your father came back to me after the war overseas. When I say I hate you I really mean I hate you, I never wanted you I only got pregnant to trap your father into marrying me and he did while I was in the first stages of my pregnancy. But when he came back all he did was cheat and leave us my hate for him spilled over into you. With each passing minute and hour I hated you more, that's why I tormented you to tear at him but he knew it. He didn't care, notice that he never offered you a home he had space, but never volunteered to take you, he wanted to continue running the streets and making babies. SO YEAH I HATE THE BOTH OF YOU MUTHAFUCKAS, NOW GET THE HELL OUT OF HERE! I WISH I NEVER HAD YOU, SHOULD HAVE HAD YOU ABORTED" Relick mom says, and shockingly spits in the face of Relick.

Everything seems to be moving in slow motion for Relick his soul is shattered he looks at his mother and is heartbroken. Shabazz covers her mouth in shock as she watches Relick she also notices the sky has completely closed and the wind has picked up followed by strange lightning and thunder. His brother and sisters smile all save Shante and his father lets his mother go. Shabazz notices that the demons are moving in for the kill as the ground begins to shake she runs to the car to get her weapons. Relick staggers a little but bursts into tears he has no words he has never known pain on this level but it all makes sense to him finally. But his mother has hit him harder than any villain that he has ever faced and the final bond has been broken he is coming. The sky turns red and orange with flames, then the demons attack.

"Yorel snaps out of it I know you are hurt but they will kill everyone here, fight damn it!" Shabazz says but he won't budge.

Shabazz takes out her sword and Nun chucks and goes to work hacking off limbs of the demons Relick still does not move. His brother tries to run but his head is ripped off and the demon forces its hand down into the headless corpse ripping out his heart through where his head once rested. Shabazz continues to battle moving with the balance and fluidity of a ballerina with deadly precision. The other sister is grabbed by the arms and legs and torn apart each limb ripped from its joint.

"YOREL MOVE THEY ARE KILLING YOUR FAMILY, SHANTE GET BEHIND ME! I'll PROTECT YOU!" Shabazz says cutting and smashing the many creatures that come their way.

Relick is having flashbacks in his mind about all the failures and obstacles his mother seems to have been behind since she disclosed how she really feels about him. The pain burns his soul tears stream down his face as he wipes the spit and tears from his face; he tries to make the choice. What reason does he have to fight; with his mother, this evil, does humanity deserve any chance? The demons run past him attacking everyone but him, his dad being ex-law enforcement unloads his gun slowing the demons down but not enough to kill them. Finally, Relick comes to the decision after the screams of his family awaken him…FIGHT!

He transforms, and his sister Shante is the only family member to notice this as he takes to the air and comes crashing down to the earth he begins to easily lay waste to the demons. However, his dad is cut to death by the many demon claws, as he tries to protect Relick's mother. His father uses everything available as a weapon, chairs, bottles, and all things handy. Then four bolts of energy strike, each materializing the form of angels. All the demons can see this and cower, trying to find an escape route, but they are incinerated with but a wave of the hand of one of the Angels. But this comes at a price it causes the gas grill next to his parents to explode his dad tries to shield his mother but they are sent flying. The family house has also been caught in the angel blast obliterating it. Just in time, Relick places a shield around his sister and Shabazz protecting them from the blast.

"NO, MY BABY GOD NOOOO SHE WAS STILL INSIDE!" Shante says as she watched the house explode with Relicks niece inside, burning cinders floating slowly to the ground.

Relick looks back in horror to where his childhood home used to be, but it is no more. He is losing so much so fast just as Mabus foretold. He can see the bodies of his brother, sister, mother, father, and niece, there is nobody to mourn. When his shield is broken by the horn of Gabriel signaling the final coming. They all fall to their knees and cover their ears as the sound wave shakes the planet. The four major Archangels line up. Azrael, Uriel, Raphael, and Gabriel gather to witness the final battle. They await the arrival of Omnipotus, Relick crawls to his parents. He turns over his father and he is dead the explosion has crushed his body and charred it. He drops his head and turns to his mother she however is still breathing, but laughing as she looks at his dad's broken body.

The sky is lit and Michael the final piece is here, Shabazz readies herself. Relick places his head on his mother's heart trying hard to fight his tears. Then suddenly they hear a voice that has to this point only uttered one word.

"Step away from that hate-filled vessel, she has allowed herself to be overcome with hate. So much to the effect that she has, destroyed the sacred bond of mother and child do not for one moment think that this will go unpunished. For you are the worst of the worst for your transgressions. Stand aside Relick we shall have our moment but for now, she must bath in divine soul cleansing fire before she is delivered to oblivion!" Omnipotous says as he bathes Relick and his mother in a blue flame but Relick has other plans.

"NO!" Relick yells while placing his shield around him and his mother.

"Are you ok, don't die, repent please so that he can see that you have a heart and you are redeemable!" Relick begs his mother; she begins to focus and grabs his hand.

"You are that young man that saved the town, me and my grandbaby a few years back. Like I said then your mother must be proud of you now?" His mother asks as she touches his face.

"I'm not sure why don't you ask her yourself?" Relick says as he deactivates his holographic facial camo.

His mother is shocked to see that the man that has been saving the world all these years is her unwanted son. She cannot find the words, because all the things she said he would not be, could not be Relick has excelled beyond her hate for him.

"Hello mother, it's your baby boy. Was hoping that I got to tell you before one of us left this Earth, but I forgive you and your anger!" Relick says as he holds her hand, but she is filled with anger and pulls away.

She is too filled with anger to say anything, his success and going beyond what she thought he could be has enraged her. She is slipping into what Omnipotus is condemning. She will be judged without mercy because she has crossed the line even here on judgment day she will not yield to her anger.

"Ma please, don't do this and say you didn't mean it. Repent take it back you can be forgiven, I don't want to lose you like this mama please!" Relick pleads but his mother will not let go, she only turns away and the hate grows within her.

The word Relick does not want to hear is spoken UNWORTHY! His mother screams as blue lights emanate from her eyes, ears, nose, and mouth. He pulls her to his chest, and she turns into salt and crumbles in his hands. Shabazz looks on and begins to cry for this is something that she rarely does, but the terrible losses Relick has received this day have momentarily penetrated her normal ironclad resolve.

"YAAAAAAAGH!" Relick screams and clutches his fist, as his mother is no more.

Shabazz runs to Relick to comfort him he cannot contain his emotions he breaks down again, but he gets angry and starts to focus.

"She knows, no matter what she felt she knows finally, but we have a job to do!" Shabazz says.

"You still feel the need to help humanity, even when your own mother gave up on you. Let this world burn stand aside let the judgment fit the many crimes of this world! Raphael replies.

"You are the few that still remain in this God-forsaken world, but it is fitting since you have sacrificed and endured so much. We will allow a few more moments to prepare for the final battle!" Gabriel says as all the Angels bow and pray.

"I knew that we would lose a lot of people but not everybody, I know I gotta dig down deep and find the internal resources to battle but I'm so tired!" Relick says as Shabazz grabs his hands.

"Not a lot left to go on I know but we have come too far to stop now win or lose, this battle is for everyone that we have lost and so much more. I am with you till the end, let us pray!" Shabazz replies as they bow their heads.

"It is only right that you are here with me at the end just like you've always been from the beginning. I thank you and want you to know that I love you, more than just as a friend!" Relick says as he touches her face, they stare into each other's eyes seeking the peace that each has brought the other for years. Then the unthinkable happens.

They kiss and the passion within it has unlocked feelings for Relick that have long since been buried. He feels that there is still hope renewed by the warmth of a woman who has moved beyond the realm of just a friend. So with that, he knows that the battle must commence, and he is ready.

"Are you ready, one last time you do know we are about to get down with Angels right!" Relick asks as he stands facing the direction of the Angels.

"Yep but we have faced worse, maybe not as powerful, but worse I was trained to follow you for just such a moment. The training has nothing to do with this now it's about my love for a person that I just can't do without, so yeah let's go!" Shabazz replies with a sword in hand.

The two stand together as the all-powerful angels stand for the final battle, but then "The Armor of GOD," is activated by Relick it is simply impressive to such a degree that even the angels bow their heads momentarily. Energy from every direction is drawn into the armor colored in silver, white, and gold. The Angels then gather enormous energy of their own at the center the focal point is Omnipotus; he channels all the energy as the planet begins to shake violently, and openings on the surface begin to open all around the city. Cars fall into them, trees and buildings begin to collapse underground pipes bursts as flames bellow through the ground.

Relick is still fueled by his charge as the world protector attacks Omnipotus punching him off his axis point he staggers and seems a bit shocked. He stands and finally, he exposes his massive powerful wings and the Sword of Truth which means the game is almost over, but not if Relick has a say.

"I have to believe we have a chance, just wish my family had just taken the time to understand me. At least one of them got to ascend, my mother was so filled with hate for me, her son no way she would be allowed into heaven. I didn't realize the sickness that held my family by the throat like that. I'm the last thing to clear our name, humanity's name!" Relick says as he focuses on the Arch Angel.

"I'm ready let's move, no time like the present let's finished this!" Shabazz replies.

"NO, YOU ARE WORTHY!" Omnipotus says as Shabazz is judged out of existence.

"DAMN IT, Omnipotus just take everyone from me?" Relick yells.

"Shabazz is most worthy and does not deserve an unfair death on this polluted planet or this battlefield!" Omnipotus replies as he ignites his flaming sword.

"What about those guys will they stay out of this, or are they gonna help you when I get the best of you!" Relick asks as the Angels all look at him while still trying to gather his composer after the quick incidents.

"This is my fight, and they are the witnesses as are you, but you are a most confident mortal!" Omnipotus says as he taps his flaming sword against his hand.

"Then you know what I always say at a time like this…WAR WITH ME!" Relick says as he pulls the Spear of Destiny out as it is struck by lightning several times.

Relick is now on the attack he charges forward Spear of Destiny pointing as if to impale Omnipotus. As the two meet each has blocked the other's attack, as there is an energy stand-off. Relick grinds his teeth and pours on energy trying to force the Archangel back. Omnipotus is faceless and shows no body emotion, he too increases his power output. The energy forces them both back through the air.

They both hover motionless as lightning strikes and thunder roars, followed by Basketball sized hail. Below on the surface building, cars are being pulverized. The ice missiles simply bounce off Relick and the Archangel. They clash again, Relick jabbing the spear-wielding it with the precision of a Zulu warrior and the spirit of OGUN, they are blocked by Omnipotus but Relick follows with a blast of blue energy from the spear knocking Omnipotous from the sky. He crashes to the surface, and Relick moves in for the kill. He is met with red flames that are two times the heat of the sun's surface, and he is totally covered in the flames. The heat cuts a path hundreds of miles in a straight line, nothing is remaining in the carved linear vector.

Omnipotus retracts the flames and lowers his sword, as there is a singular smoldering area. The Archangel stands observing the area, and Relick emerges still burning but protected by the Armor of God. To the surprise of Omnipotus, Relick charges again holding the spear like a bow staff.

He strikes the legs and head of Omnipotus, and he staggers back but Relick is not done. He then uses the spear as a pole vault and dropkicks, the staggering Omnipotus. Omnipotus is sent swirling off his feet but never touches the ground as his wings slow his rate to a halt. Miles from the original battle point, Relick places The Spear of Destiny on his back, Omnipotus does the same. They engage in hand-to-hand combat, Omnipotus lands the first blow, he shockwave slaps

Relick to the ground, and Relick quickly responds with a shattering elbow to the jaw. The Archangel wraps both arms around Relicks mid-section and leaps into the air. Relick slams elbow after thunderous elbow between the wings and shoulder blades of Omnipotus. They turn mid-flight as Omnipotus throws Relick to the ground, and streaks to him smashing his foot into the face of the downed Relick. He begins to grind his foot into the face of Relick and stomps immediately following the face grinding. Relick grabs Omnipotus by the ankle and forces him into an ankle lock. Relick then flips Omnipotus onto his stomach still applying pressure to his ankle. Relick begins to stomp his foe to the back of the head, with his ankle lock still applied he, lifts Omnipotus and slams him to the ground twice before releasing him.

"You are a most worthy opponent, only one mortal has ever provided me with such a worthy battle with these new weapons you would seem on par with me!" Omnipotus says.

"Well let me see if I can't put you on your back, for the one, two, three. How does that sound Klondike?" Relick asks as he slowly walks towards, the Archangel pressing his fist into his hand.

The basketball-sized hail is still slamming into the surface and the Archangel increases its repetitive barrage. The solid balls of destruction whip past the ears of Relick but then some begin to strike him knocking him off balance. Relick takes to punch the chunks of frozen water they shatter as Relick makes sure the shrapnel flies in the direction of Omnipotus. They simply evaporate before striking him, to Relick's surprise his armor is now providing him the same protection.

"Let us see how you fare with an all-out environmental assault!" The Archangel says.

"Don't sing it, bring it!" Relick responds as he is hit with even larger boulder-sized hail, and he begins to stagger.

The ground begins to shake slowly then violently, the other Archangels watch on unmoved, and undisturbed only for the moment following the action by simply turning their heads in the direction of the battle. Huge portions of rock and Earth are ripped up, and slam into Relick from all directions. He tries to take to the air but larger ice boulders pound him forcing him down, but the ground is also assaulting him so he is flipped over and over through the air. He is disoriented as and tries desperately to get his bearings he is met with lightning shocking him. To add more damage to the warrior, he is hit with a blue flame beam. Relick then falls from the sky and to the ground and is covered with tons of rock and ice. Realizing that in this battle if you are immobilized for a few moments it is game over.

Relick tunnels underneath the ground and uppercuts the Archangel, sending him sprawling backward. As Omnipotus staggers backward Relick grabs him by the wing and punches him repeatedly in what should be his face. He then still holding his wing spins him faster and faster and flings him through the air and out of sight. Relick falls to one knee for the moment and looks around at the surrounding area. The area has been devastated, lava begins to spew from the Earth, he then looks at the angels and shakes his head; he is filled with thoughts of his loved ones. He stands filled with anger and sorrow in one jump he is airborne and streaks off in the direction that he threw Omnipotus. He locates the Archangel, and he is just hovering motionless in the sky.

"I got all day, what about you huh?" Relick questions.

"Your kind has had far too long, a pity you have no more time despite your misconception of the given statement you've made!" Omnipotous responds as he spreads his enormous wings in all their glory, and attacks Relick.

The attack is sudden and powerful; Relick has no way to block the assault. He is knocked to the surface. The blows and speed of the two, send them smashing into different continents across the planet. They land in the amazon rainforest, Relick smacks Omnipotus with a huge tree, clearing acres of lush growth, and the remaining animals scatter trying to find cover. Relick drives the tree into the impenetrable body of his foe, forcing him into the ground the massive tree splinters. Dirt seems unable to cling to the skin of the Archangel, and Relick begins to ground and pound him. Omnipotus returns the favor and administers the same attack style, only the armor has protected Relick to this point.

"You have relied on the God Armor to protect you from my physical assaults, but let me introduce your being to a different attack mortal!" Omnipotus says as he holds Relick head down in a small but slightly deep body of water enough to drown normal mortals if held down long enough.

Relick struggles but only for a moment; he is quickly yanked by the neck and held up in the air. Then slammed down again onto dry land, Omnipotus with one hand held high draws in a dark fog-like substance. He shoves his hand into the mouth of Relick, and the thick dark fog substance jets down the arm of Omnipotus and into the mouth and lungs of Relick. The force is like that of a fire extinguisher; the armor forms a helmet that almost cuts off the hand of the Arch Angel. So he tosses Relick across the surface, and he can no longer breathe the helmet is sealed.

It is preventing anything to enter Relicks body; Relick then turns and looks at Omnipotus. Hovering low over a mud bank, wings extended as he silently watches Relick battle for air.

"Did you think this was a game, mortal this is what I do when my father has had enough? You mortals with your petty evils have infected the balance of the universe. Because you are one of his greatest creations, you are one of his biggest disappointments in all of the cosmos of all timelines. With all of the chances he has allowed you, and your kind sees fit to spit on his mercy. I SAY NO MORE!" Omnipotus says as he draws his flaming sword of GOD.

He is the only Angel to receive such a weapon handcrafted from GOD. Relick finally opens the helmet and begins to regurgitate the black fumes, as he crawls the substance turns into a thick tar. It eats all the way through the surface and does not stop. He wipes away the thick strings of saliva that clings to his lips, as Omnipotus moves in closer he gets a shock.

Relick with blinding speed hurls the Destiny Spear, in slow motion, it penetrates the chest of Omnipotus and exists through his back he falls to the surface. White illuminating light explodes from his wound. The spear circles back making a whistling sound but in a blurring move, Omnipotus deflects it with the flaming sword. It returns to Relick and he stands renewed with confidence because now it's on.

"Just when you thought you'd seen the best humanity had to offer, you wake up with a big smoking hole in ya ass. Looks like you are gonna need stitches, and a big ass bandage!" Relick taunts as Omnipotus stands the white light energy stops and the hole closes but not completely on his chest or his back.

His wing appeared to be damaged by the spear attack, but it is quite obvious that he does not truly need it to fly. As he stands he begins to float as if nothing has changed with his ability to manipulate gravity. Relick grabs tight on the base and near the tip of the Spear of Destiny. Waiting to embrace the battle that has pushed him to the brink.

"I have never been injured before by a mortal or any being I have fought in battle not even Lucifer, this is unprecedented and most unexpected. You fight as though you have all of creation on your shoulders, why do you carry such a burden? Would this be the same if you had no powers, would you fight so valiantly if the contents in my question were so?" Omnipotus asks squeezing the GOD sword; it turns to a color of ionized blue.

"Yeah, of course, I would I come from a people that have been fighting for four hundred plus years, beat down deprived, infected, mislead, murdered, raped, brought over in chains physically and mentally we had no voice. We fought back even when we had nothing, but the will to fight. We prayed to GOD for help and it seemed that he didn't hear us but today it seems that he did, he chose me to be the one that battled for us all. Forged in fire, and blood he produced a metal that was unstoppable. I know you didn't think that this weapon that could pierce the skin of Christ couldn't do the same to your rusty butt, now that's just arrogant. I WILL NOT STOP, GET THAT STRAIGHT!" Relick yells to Omnipotus.

"So be it!" Omnipotus yells as he swings the mighty sword in the direction of Relick.

Relick barely dodges a huge wave of energy that takes the form of an enormous sickle. The energy is so powerful from the sword, that it blinds Relick and cuts part of South America off. The gash is so deep that it seems to go to the floor of the Atlantic Ocean. As the ocean empties into the crevasse static sparks off from the dark opening resembling a form of lighting. Relick simply hovers with his jaw dropped at the immense power of the sword and Omnipotus.

The slash gash seems to go on forever as Relick can no longer see the end; he can only track the beginning.

"Do you see the power, this is what I have done to countless self-righteous civilizations across the dimensions. All wiped out but your pitiful Godless race, that has chosen the path of so many to die!" Omnipotus says.

"Well some of us fight and fought for GOD, doesn't that count for something? We all didn't fail because we didn't try; we failed because the evil was to win it was written. To take dominion over this planet, didn't stop some of us from trying, as many bad cards we had stacked against us. We have lost everything in this war I love and respect my GOD, and I will die defending the planet. So if this is my end, I will die here, right here with the rest of them and I didn't want to defend them all but here I stand. I will battle the way that GOD would have wanted me to, why he created me this is my time. SO SHUT THE HELL UP AND LET'S GO! Relick says as he holds out his hand and the spear flips into his hand pulsating with enormous energy!

They clash with humongous power at their command; the released forces have begun wreaking havoc on the entire planet, land, air, and water. The remaining life is being killed off. Omnipotus slashes down hard with his sword Relick continues to block each slash instinctively. Relick counters with jabs with the spear, his attack is also blocked and the high piercing metallic clang of the two weapons is earsplitting.

The Archangel lands a foot on the face of Relick, but swiftly his foot is grabbed by Relick and our warrior releases a powerful blast of energy into the body of Omnipotus. Sending him skipping across the Pacific Ocean, he makes contact with the non-inhabited Hawaiian Islands with a resonating thud. Relick focuses a tight beam from the Spear of Destiny at Omnipotus yelling at the top of his voice as if trying to deliver a knockout punch. Screaming for all of humanity and the terrible losses he and the universe have faced today. The Archangel sees the power assault bearing down and closes his wings around his body for protection, there is a flash and an explosion that resembles the detonation of a nuclear warhead.

The mushroom cloud rises high as Relick floats above it waiting for the cloud to disperse. He is impressed as this new power, has given him hope but ever so slightly, each blow sends each of the two flying miles from each point of contact.

"Man, I hit him pretty hard that was one helluva blast. Glad I don't have to hold back anymore there are no more people or animals on Earth left, all the islands of Hawaii are gone. All this power now I'm beginning to see and understand why GOD is tired of us this is no joke. The arrogance of us!" Relick says still clutching the Spear of Destiny tightly preparing, waiting, and hoping it is all over finally.

"I am a HOSTILE JUDGE, not Louis Ortiz. I am not here to make friends; I am here to bring ends! Omnipotus says but it seems to resonate with the entire crumbling planet.

Then a form rises from the incredible mushroom cloud, it shimmers as a star would then the wings and humanoid form takes shape. Relick sighs and gets prepared to battle.

"So you must be a Lebron Lames fan, you know every title he got was rigged. From the Spurs to Golden State, if you gonna be mad then why not take it out on the association? Zap him in the ass with lightning, give him something really to flop or whine about. Man, you could have turned him into a platypus, problem solved. That's really what you are mad about right?" Relick distracts as he tries to buy time for a counter-attack.

"ENOUGH PRATTLE, YOUR ENTIRE SOCIAL STRUCTURE IS POSITION TO EVERYTHING THAT YOU COME IN CONTACT WITH!" Omnipotus replies.

"Ouch, man, just saying you acting like I just told you to spank your bad son that was acting up in a supermarket. Oh, did I just tell on you?" Relick taunts, he then plows into the Archangel forcing him to block the assault.

The seas boil and the lands shake as they take their battle to the surface of Australia. Relick attacks from above punching Omnipotus through the land, and he follows as the battle takes place underground. It goes deeper and deeper as they borrow into ancient caverns; lava erupts and spills on the combatants. They are unaffected, but Relick is sent flying through walls of solid rock and then thrown out of the underground battlefield. He is launched high into the sky, but the Archangel summons a blue beam of energy from the clouds striking Relick. He flips over and over before making contact with the surface and the beam is then focused on him pinning him to the surface. The pressure is causing the land to buckle beneath him; he struggles to get the Spear of Destiny in his hand to counter the effect.

So Relick begins to concentrate and the spear spins from his back like a propeller. It spins so fast that it blocks the beam as Relick fires a desperate beam of his own striking, and catching Omnipotus completely off guard taking the blast full force and bringing him to all fours dropping the sword. The sword sticks to the ground as it begins to do irreparable damage to the landscape. With his mind Relick causes the Spear of Destiny to pop Omnipotus as he retrieves his sword, he is sent flying. Relick flies and tackles him in mid-air; the spear is met by the sword as they battle. They streak across the Pacific Ocean battling ferociously; occasionally they touch uncharted islands that are destroyed under the weight of the battle.

Then as two small dots, they streak off with end trails of smoke, hurling energy blasts from their hands and their respective weapons. Australia the incredible outback is bombarded with projectiles of power. Relick appears in front of Omnipotus, and lands a massive uppercut, and as Omnipotus reaches the Apex of his ascent Relick catches him with an elbow to the back of the head smashing him into the surface.

"I'm starting to get the hang of this armor, this is some bad ass weapon!" Relick says as he looks to the outback surface looking for his opponent.

He then is thrown to the other side of the outback slamming into Ayers Rock. Half of it comes crumbling down on top of him. Hundreds of tons of rock seemingly stop Relick in his movement, but not for long. He pulverizes huge boulders as he emerges from his temporary tomb; he then slings a massive slab of rock at Omnipotous.

Even though he was cloaked, Relick still could see him thanks to "The Armor of God."

The archangel falls to the ground pinned by the enormous slab, he too is not held long. His sword cuts through the material like butter.

" I believe you have learned much from the Akashic records, this is still very impressive. For your kind can only understand, savagery, violence, and brutality. Universally it takes a kind and fair soul to understand such knowledge; your kind normally would only use such power for personal gains. Interesting to speak in the least format?" Omnipotus says.

"Well, why didn't you angels do the job of watching over people, protecting them from this madness that, is or was humanity? Oh, that's right free will, I really don't want to talk anymore we are past all that mess!" Relick says as bits of rock continue to fall behind him from the mountain.

"Indeed!" The archangel says.

The two again meet and clash causing untold damage to the outback, when Omnipotus slings down his sword. The immeasurable power at his command cuts a third of the continent away. Although Relick dodges it he is flung out violently, flipping head over heels, toward Africa. The last image that he sees is the massive land that slowly sinks into the boiling ocean.

"How can anything be so powerful, what am I saying this is one of the hands of GOD here. The only reason that I'm still here is because of the armor, but here I've been knocked clean over to Africa. Just by the mere shockwave, from the energy that I was barely able to dodge." Relick says as he gathers himself, but he cannot locate the archangel.

He notices that the continent of Africa is not on fire, at least no part that he can detect, that will soon change as he can hear the familiar buzz that is associated with the sword Omnipotus carries. Another less powerful blade of energy just barely misses Relick, and he flies towards the Sahara desert trying to spare the remaining wildlife on Earth from the colossal battle. He is followed by blade after blade of energy, obliterating everything behind him as he flies away dodging with incredible speed.

Relick is very near his destination and is clipped by one of the energy blasts in the leg. He is knocked off his flight pattern and is brought to an abrupt halt. Omnipotus hovers overhead with his sword drawn when suddenly he speaks.

"For a mortal, you are most formidable I will give you that, maybe my father has a point about…some of you, but that will not change my mission. You still fight for a species that must be eradicated. There are no humans, left, and yet you still fight, this is puzzling?" Omnipotus says.

"Well you are right there is no one left, but I fight for him, my spiritual father, your father. This is what he put inside of me, to fight, to do something when there is nothing left to fight for but the last breath in my body. To battle for those who cannot, to punch injustice in the nose, and to body slam those that want to enslave and oppress. Until the evil that lives in the hearts of humanity is purged outta the souls here or anywhere that I come in contact with!" Relick replies while spitting sand.

"I am not evil, I am a force of nature and now I will show you power again on a scale that you cannot imagine. I will put a little distance so that you can see the scale of what power truly is!" Omnipotus says as he streaks across the desert and lands on the surface.

"Yeah, yeah you've been showing us all for fifty-two weeks or better. Now, what other trick could you possibly show me, Mister not evil? Because you sure seem to have evil phases to me?" Relick asks.

"Behold mortal this is true power!" Omnipotus says, he raises his hand and slams it down on the surface of the sand.

The sand explodes upwards, one hundred feet, two hundred feet, and then it simply turns into miles high. A wall so high and wide that Relick cannot see the beginning or the end, and the wind begins to pick up. The most powerful sand storm in the history of man has begun, as the sand particles hit like projectiles flung from a rail gun.

The few remaining animals left on the planet try to escape, only to have their skin peeled, from their bones. Whether in the air or on the ground and in a flash feathers and bone are grinded away. Relick closes the faceplate on the armor and draws the Spear of Destiny.

"NOW THIS IS A NEW TRICK, DAMN!" Relick yells as the force of the storm increases, as he runs at superhuman speed trying to stay ahead of the sand storm, but the storm is too fast.

Relick places the Spear of Destiny in front and erects a force field trying to buy some time to plan. But he will be given none, for the archangel fires energy and the shield. Weakened by the power assault, Omnipotus speed blitz the shield shattering it. Relick is knocked back as the towering sand wall begins to crash down on him with tons of force, he tries to take to the air and fight through the curtain of sand but is blinded and soundly knocked back to the earth. The speeding Omnipotus is relentless in his attack, and Relick can no longer track him even with his enhanced abilities. He is struck from every angle, and unable to block or defend against the attacks. Then suddenly he remembers that he has to focus, and allow the armor to help in this battle so he does.

So deep is his focus that, the ferocious storm raging becomes silent. He is completely still; as time seems to slow down, then on the next pass Relick grabs the archangel by the wing. Relick yanks him back, and repeatedly knees his foe in the face, each blow sounds like thunder, and then tosses him into the sand storm wall. He disappears behind the sand curtain.

"I gotta remember to focus, this armor will take years to master. It has so many, abilities I've gotta slow down!" Relick says as he probes the area where Omnipotus was thrown and now vanished.

The sand resembles a waterfall, or cloud, surrounded by a deafening sound that in itself, jars the soul. Without a warning, Relicks armor is penetrated and his right leg is impaled. He is shocked, and grunts deeply, as the sand begins to enter his wound like a band saw, he is forced to turn his back shielding the wound. He begins to focus through the great pain, and Omnipotus tackles him. Relick digs his feet into the ground and his movement is stopped, he quickly grabs the archangel. He pulls his enemy by the back of the head, kneeing him in the face repeatedly once again. Locking his arms under the shoulder of Omnipotus, Relick streaks into the sky with him in tow.

They plow through the sky until they are even higher than the massive sandstorm wall. Entering into space Relick notices that the sun is dying and that there are no stars only a black void. The millions of twinkling lights that once filled the heavens have all been blown out as if they were mere candles. Angered at the apparent death of all things, he spins in a circle and slings Omnipotus into the moon. So violent is the impact that the moon is split in two. Relick pursues the archangel smashing through the newly created debris field. He lands on the split moon surface, at first he experiences the difference in gravity, and the armor automatically makes the adjustment for him.

"Where are you, this ain't over. You are gonna pay for what you have done, is this what you want? Look out there, there is nothing left! LOOK DAMN YOU! Relick yells the armor has allowed his voice to be heard even in the vacuum of space.

"THIS IS THE FAULT OF MAN, I AM THE JANITOR WHEN YOU BAD KIDS MESS UP THE PLAYGROUND. DEAL WITH IT! Omnipotus replies as he slams his fist into Relick's jaw, stunning him momentarily.

Angered Relick grabs two enormous pieces of broken moon surface with each hand and crushes the archangel between them. The moon rocks are the size of the Great Pyramid of Giza easily. Relick with great strength applies more pressure; the archangel shatters them both and is free. He grabs Relick by the throat and takes him back to the atmosphere of the earth. The two trade blows through the earth's protective atmosphere, they don't even notice the extreme heat of the frictional build-up. They pass through clouds and are cooled the two are accompanied by the crumbling moon chunks, then they collide back to where the battle originated.

The sand storm and towering sand wall have not diminished one bit, as they continue to battle. Omnipotus with a thunderous kick strikes Relick in the injured leg and then vanishes. In incredible pain, Relick grabs the leg probing the area, as moon rocks smash all around him. The planet Earth is dying and shakes violently, it begins to break apart.

"Where the hell did he go this time, he is just full of tricks?" Relick asks and gets an immediate answer.

He can see Omnipotus coming, so he draws his spear and throws it with all of his might. It seemed to be on target until Omnipotus make a right-angle turn dodging it. Relick is shocked, and this momentary lapse in focus gives Omnipotus the opening he's been waiting on. Time seems to slow down as he drives his sword through the armor and deep into the chest of Relick. Relick tries to remove the blade with both hands, the pain is excruciating. As Omnipotus drives it deeper and pins Relick to the sand surface.

"It is over, the battle is mine yield as if you really had a choice or stood a chance!" Omnipotus boasts, standing over the fallen Relick who begins to bleed out.

"There is always a chance, always!" Relick says as he fires his last powerful energy blast at the overconfident archangel.

The blast catches him square in the face, staggering backward a bit. Relick raises his hand summoning the spear to him. Omnipotus spreads his mighty wing about to deliver the final blow. When "The Spear of Destiny" opens up the back of his skull penetrates his head through his face. Energy erupts from his body and he falls face first into the sand only to be propped up by the protruding spear like a bicycle kickstand.

"In the words of Tacea, CHECKMATE MUTHAFUCKA!" Relick says in a weakened voice.

Then he musters up a scornful yell, "THAT'S FOR SHABAZZ, MY NIECE, MY TEAM, MY FAMILY, THE UNIVERSES, MY MOTHER!" As he stands he closes his eyes tightly, in pain beyond emotional pain!

The massive sand storm wall comes crashing down exposing an incredibly lost ancient city. There is a calming silence that has come over the battlefield; a sudden wind passes by the ears of Relick. He looks at the once-covered ancient city in awe; he then pulls the sword from his chest with great pain and falls to his knees.

He looks at the fallen angel, and then there is a stir of sand and energy. The other archangels appear surrounding their fallen brother. They all look in the direction of Relick and take Michael and begin to dematerialize. But before they finally leave, they nod giving their approval of a battle well fought. Relick sticks the sword in the sand, reaches, and does the same with the Spear of Destiny.

Relick staggers to the edge of the city holding his chest to see the incredible advanced African city. But he is stunned because all around him he can see more and more, massive cities that have long since been buried by the ancient sands, in the distance as well as far as the eye can see. History that was once covered is now uncovered by Omnipotus, unfortunately, he is the only living being anywhere left to witness this incredible sight. He is met by a blinding light, and he feels as though he is dying which is obvious and is the last human, the last man standing, and the last living life form in the universe he fought for everything and lost everything except his humanity and faith. He sees through the blinding light huge wings, he thinks the worst, as he knows he cannot fight another battle. But he will not stand down as he prepares for battle.

"God, give me the resolve to overcome this because I can not do this alone, I never could!" Relick prays when the archangel Raphael approaches him.

"You have represented life well, no living entity has ever defeated Michael even though each before you had a weapon that would allow them to do so. Allow me to heal your wounds!" Raphael touches Relick and heals all his wounds and steps back as a powerful voice erupts and speaks to Relick in a calm manner. The voice is accompanied by a brilliant and beautiful light, and the incredible presentation begins.

"Making the choices you have, you have achieved "Summum Bonum." You have met the requirements that all living beings, seeking purity, peace, and a righteous existence strive to have." The light says, speaking in a manner that causes Relick to take a knee.

The energy that he feels is all too familiar; it is the energy of the Supreme Creator. Relick cannot even raise his head, for though he has battled odds, no living mortal has ever faced and triumphed. Worth is not a title he is willing to wear; he believes that no mortal is worthy to look upon the energy of the divine. He is no exception no matter what he has done.

"As stated in ancient Kemet, they were the first to receive and understand these teachings. Man is divided into three stages, lovers of wealth, lovers of honor, and lovers of wisdom. The last being the most important, once a man has understood these facts and chosen the right paths purification and salvation of the soul follow. You have always held on to the importance of honor and wisdom, forsaking the temptation of wealth. Paths are not easily followed by man's majority, but you have always upheld these virtues. This propelled you to "Summum Bonum" which means godlike, your lower nature never rivaled your higher nature, which provided you with a harmonious balance with the universe truly remarkable. I am here to give you two choices; because these steps you have taken all your life have evolved you to a divine status. Today your soul has been purified, and your transformation is complete. So rise my son for few have attained such a level anywhere in the universe." The supreme says.

"So what happens now, what does it all mean? There is nothing left anywhere and the planet is burned just like it says in the bible purified by fire?" Relick says as he unwillingly; tries to peek at the humanoid form that slowly takes shape in the blinding light.

"You have two choices, ascend with me and the angels learn about all, or restore all as it was only to repeat the cycle anew. If you chose to restart all, I will allow you to retain the memories of what has happened. It will be a burden that you will bare alone, and you will be. Here however is energy, positive energy from your past. Your Great Grandmother, she wanted to speak to you this shall be allowed!" The Supreme says.

"Baby how are you, seems that you have been busy and I always knew you had great things ahead for you. I am so proud as I have watched you from beyond grow into a fine, strong young man! His grandmother says as she takes solid form.

"Grandma I'm so glad to see you, so much I wanted to say so many things I should have done when you were with us. I feel as though I didn't appreciate you, I'm so sorry for that, I have missed you so much!" Relick says as they embraced one another, he becomes choked up.

"It's ok, you were never a disrespectful child and that's all I could ask, sorry for your mother's treatment of you baby. But now you have a very tough choice ahead of you, and I don't have much time left so

I will leave you to it. This world has the potential to be better, but won't the new orange U.S. president would have opened up a real whopper had all this not happened!" She says as she kisses Relicks forehead and releases his hands.

His Great Grandmother begins to fade just as she appeared.

Relick ponders all the questions; in his mind, he has grown tired of the cruelty of humanity. The denial, lies, and the history of man, as evolution continues to mutate all of the horrible things that should have been forgotten. They are simply transferred, generation after generation. The human condition does it have the ability to change or is it exactly like what lies before him, simply headed into ruin time after time regardless of the chances? He begins to think of family, friends, then the smile of Shabazz.

Metatron the largest of all the angels appears extends his enormous hand and the remaining angels land in it taking their leave.

With that Gabriel blows his mighty horn, it vibrates throughout the multiverse, and Relick stands. He tilts his head toward the heavens eyes closed inhaling slowly and deeply. He begins to rise and float from the battle-scared surface bathed in the glow of the Supreme, and the armor of GOD slowly fades from his body.

There are no birds, nothing in the air, nothing at all left! Relick says.

Suddenly there in the sky above him is a huge black flamming bird, it streaks across the sky and quickly into space letting out an powerful shriek, causing a sonic boom upon it's departure, finally his decision is made!